BEING
WORK

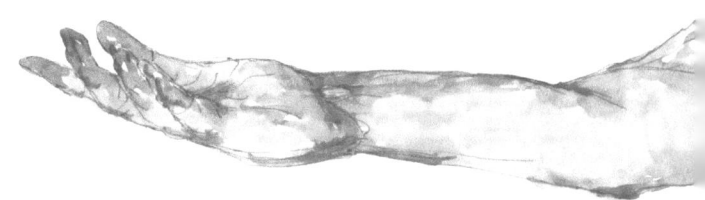

Being Work
©Dorothy Dubrule, 2024

Copyright of individual essays attributed to their respective authors.

Insert Press
ISBN: 978-1-947322-14-1
Library of Congress Control Number: 2023952327

Cover Design by Gil Omry-Barel

Cover image *Arm Being Work* by Eileen Wolf Echikson

Acknowledgements:
In addition to the contributors, I'd like to express deep appreciation for the avid advocates of this book, including Asher Hartman, who connected me with Insert Press and Kate Banford who introduced me to Eileen. Thank you to my performance community and the pals who so consistently and generously encouraged me, inspired me, sent emails on my behalf, amplified the project and gave me the confidence to believe in myself, despite many bouts of imposter syndrome. And lastly, thank you to my family and to Jared, for lifting me up sky-high and making my laugh lines run deep. I am so grateful to be in it with you.

What I'm doing when I'm selling out, Dorothy Dubrule's essay beginning on page 90, was originally commissioned by the San Francisco Museum of Modern Art's digital publication, Open Space, for the spring 2019 season. Thanks to editors Claudia La Rocco and Gordon Faylor.

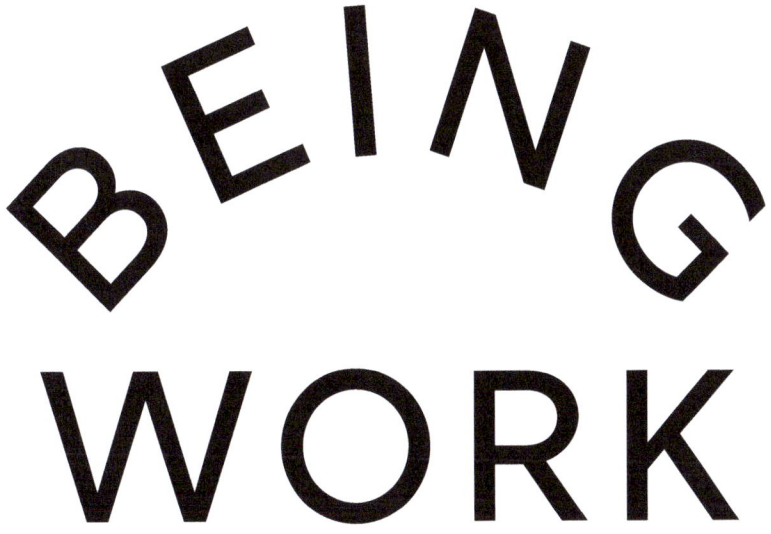

BEING WORK

Edited by Dorothy Dubrule

Essays by effie bowen, Casey Brown, Dorothy Dubrule, Jessica Emmanuel, Paul Hamilton, Allie Hankins, Kestrel Farin Leah and Mireya Lucio.

Illustrations by Eileen Wolf Echikson.

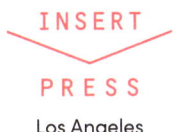

INSERT PRESS

Los Angeles

Contents

6   Introduction by Dorothy Dubrule

18   Mireya Lucio

28   Casey Brown

36   Jessica Emmanuel

48   Kestrel Farin Leah

58   Allie Hankins

68   effie bowen

80   Paul Hamilton

90   Dorothy Dubrule

102   Contributor Biographies

109   List of Illustrations

Introduction

Dorothy Dubrule

I'm on a family trip to Minneapolis, heels clomping through the hard, white halls of the Walker Art Center after a year of wondering, maybe even fantasizing, about never setting foot in a museum again. The exhibition on view, *Paradox of Stillness*, examines the overlaps and spaces between sculpture and performance. Many of the works included point to an absence of human activation, like a pedestal from Piero Manzoni called *Base magica—Sculptura vivente*, whose wall text states that it "transforms any person, any object placed on it, [into] a work of art." I watch my mother take an athletic step onto the tall pedestal and stand there, thoughtfully, waiting. Other pieces have live components, like the man sitting on a chair, walled in by three suspended copper sheets that hover a couple of feet off the ground. This man is *not* a nescient gallery visitor behaving badly, but a paid performer who has been cast to sit there. Francesco Arena's *Angolo scontento (Hommage à la mort de Sigmund Freud)* is activated by a person who was born in 1939, the same year as Sigmund Freud's death. The wall text states that, when approached, the person sitting inside will "begin a conversation, revealing fragments of their life."

Curious about the composition of Arena's conversational score, I say hello. The man greets me with a smile and states his name and his birth year (1939), followed by silence. I introduce myself, and another pause settles between us. After a moment, I ask about the process to learn the piece. Through giggles, he shares that his one-time rehearsal was supposed to have been two hours but ended up taking only minutes. The single directive was to say his name and birth year. In an effort to extend our exchange, I make a comment about the awkward height of the copper triangle that surrounds him, and how it means he can only see the feet of gallery visitors all day. He replies that he is never bored, and in fact, was delightfully surprised the first time he received a paycheck from the museum. He would have been happy to volunteer. He adds that he thinks this piece should happen all over the place, not just museums. "Why not the Mall of America? It's great because strangers talk to each other." I feel warmed by his sense of pride at being a part of this exhibit. I am reminded that it is a privilege to be seen as a work of art. It is a joy to connect with fellow humans, while held within the confines of an art experience. I think of the many conversations I've had with colleagues in performance circling this topic: untangling bouts of resentment and shame, the restless desire for more directives than the work offers, and the oxymoron of being both seen and nullified, at once valued and ignored—the vulnerability of objectification. What if we could all experience the bare gratitude of this eighty-two year old man? I glance over at two young, femme-presenting performers in skin-tight body suits that match the tapestry they lay on, "like a painting come to life." They are posed languidly, each holding feminist theory books in front of an image of Karl Marx's grave (Goshka Macuga's *Death of Marxism, Women of All Lands Unite*). I imagine dropping them into the Mall of America.

But the swirl of daydreams evoked by a museum visit, even after a pandemic year spent in isolation, cannot wrest my mind from where it has been. I'm experiencing a lapse of faith in the wake of the dramatic loss of the world we used to live in, the unfoldings and reckonings of the uprisings for racial justice, and the inescapable impetus to face ubiquitous systemic inequity; to see the way things are for how they have been all along. As a dancer, performance-maker and director of a non-profit platform for dance and performance in Los Angeles, I am afraid to acknowledge that, more often than not these days, I find myself lacking conviction that performance is something worth returning to. At a time of mourning and revelation, my dedication to performance feels lost in the tide of ongoing pandemic conditions. It has become a painful remembrance of something that used to set the rhythms of my calendar with weighty importance, and now feels futile and hollow.

One afternoon in 2018, I met a dancer friend for coffee and sandwiches between rehearsals and shared an idea I had for a book. At the time, I had been working my way through a string of odd performance jobs in various galleries and museums. I was roaming around an opening gala with a sheet over my head, like a Halloween ghost, for hours until museum staff tracked me down to tell me I was off the clock, and found me hiding from a philanthropist's dog, who had been voraciously hunting my body parts under the sheet; I was all but naked with a merkin and a mask on, my legs folded over the shoulders of a sex doll, watching two old white men, each dressed as Morpheus from the Matrix, discuss how the piece I was a part of was "great, but where would you put it?"; I was all but naked with my underwear on, posing as a stripping museum guard, lurking in the last gallery of a large group exhibition; I was fully naked in a stark white gallery, recounting my earliest memories of snow in a self-induced trance state. I loved collecting these snapshots of surreal circumstances, and at the same time felt uncomfortably aware that they far outnumbered my stories of paid dance work. I wondered what the value of this strange kind of labor was, to my fellow performers and to the throngs of gallery visitors (in remarkable contrast to the size of the average dance show audience). When exhibitions closed, I wondered how this work would be remembered. I wondered how *we* would be remembered.

    Since that initial conversation, I've worked on this collection in fits and starts over five years, and published writing on my museum-guard-stripper experience, which you can find in these pages. Through the pandemic and its many false endings, this project began to feel increasingly like a before-times relic without much to say about where we are now, and so I've shelved it many times. An obsessive part of me (the dancer part of me, one of my contributors might say) always nags me back. I've realized that it is not only a matter of work ethic, but, at its core, the sincere relationships between myself and the contributing artists that have driven me to complete this project. Between Mireya Lucio, Casey Brown, Jessica Emmanuel, Kestrel Leah, Allie Hankins, effie bowen, myself and Paul Hamilton, performers from the dance and theater worlds have shared their experiences taking up the work of Marina Abramović,

Maria Hassabi, Julien Prévieux, Gordon Hall, Narcissister, Bruce Nauman and Tino Sehgal, respectively. In collecting their stories, I have been trusted to assemble portraits of the talents, desires, anxieties, humor, and pain of my colleagues. My fervor for matters of performance may feel distant, but the earnest writing each performer has shared remains imbued with pulsing, vibrating life. Lapse of faith aside, to have even three pages of access to the soft parts of another person's internal world is an undeniable magic, in and of itself.

With the accounts of just eight performers included, this collection is not intended to be a survey, but rather, a sampling that points to the epic iceberg of stories that remain untold. At the same time, I don't mean to suggest that the pool of performers in the field of western experimental performance is vast. It can often feel more like a tide pool (as indicated by the number of overlaps in cast from project to project). But there are many performance traditions and social identities that are not represented here.

Early on, it felt important to set specific parameters for the contents of the collection: personal narratives that depict the experience of mounting live work in a visual arts context (gallery, museum, art fair), works designed for visual arts contexts, conceptualized independent of a collaborative process with performers, with the work often already having been performed by another cast in another site, and accounts authored by people who identify as trained performers.

Within these narrowed boundaries, I encountered further challenges in soliciting writing from fellow performers. Amongst workers in a gig economy, a skill set designed for the short-term can develop when one must adapt to and then let go of constructed worlds in rapid succession. For many, the memories of past gigs were long gone, or never fully formed in the first place. Additionally, an already significant amount of writing on the tension between performance and visual art precedes this project. I recommend: Sarah

Wookey's *Open Letter to Artists*, written in response to the MOCA gala described in the first essay of this collection, an event which, for many, broke open the conversation about working conditions for performers in museums; *Critical Correspondence: Dance and the Museum*, conceived and curated by Nicole Daunic and Abigail Levine; Claire Bishop's essay, *Black Box, White Cube, Gray Zone: Dance Exhibitions and Audience Attention*; and *On Value*, edited by Ralph Lemon and Triple Canopy, to start. The topic can easily feel tired, and cursorily summarized by the absences of sufficient pay and a green room.

This dismissal does not speak to the complexity of our conditions. In Los Angeles, where I am based, museums and galleries are far more likely to pay dancers than (non-commercial) choreographers, and performing artists will get higher commissions from visual arts institutions than our (few) performance institutions. With theater budgets dwindling, performance seems to have a more stable future housed within visual art spaces, though their foundations are not unshakeable, either. Having ushered thousands of excited visitors through interactive water and light-based environments, Random International's *Rain Room* and James Turrell's *Ganzfeld*, at the Los Angeles County Museum of Art, and noting the proliferation of installation-based work (often with scheduled "activations") on exhibit, I see visual art spaces spaces catering to patrons interested in the kinds of personalizable, visceral experiences live work offers. With stability to be gained on all sides, it is time to attend to the performers who hold the tension of this ill-fitting union most intimately.

This project is not motivated by an attempt to condemn artists or art institutions, though criticisms can of course be extracted from the stories the collection contains. Given a history of call-outs via published accounts of labor conditions, a performer who writes can represent a threat... though prevailing power dynamics in visual arts spaces overwhelmingly favor the primary artist and institution over any performer. As a result, contracts for live exhibitions may contain a non-disclosure agreement, and some performers I reached out to were not comfortable writing because of a sense of responsibility to these contracts, or fear of jeopardizing future work opportunities with the artist or institution. A further complication is that performers are not necessarily also writers. Some of the essays included here are compositions of transcribed conversations, to provide more ease in putting text to experience. For many, writing is reserved for the necessity of securing funding for a performance project. This brings me to perhaps the biggest hurdle for this collection: I had no compensation to offer my contributors. Those who did choose to participate have been incredibly generous with their time and efforts, but a lot of performers are not in the position to volunteer their time. I cannot overstate my appreciation for the seven who waded into murky water with me and bobbed along in the waves of this project's stops and starts, through the many small and large shifts in each of their lives.

Allie, Casey, effie, Jessica, Kestrel, Mireya and Paul are writing from disparate performance communities across the United States and Europe, as well as divergent places in their performance careers. Yet there is a great deal of repetition in what they describe and how they describe it. While editing each contribution I found that the writing continually demonstrated a challenge of verb tense. Undoubtedly, this is the nature of writing from distant memories: the distinction between past and present dissolves. I wonder if there is also a connection to the nature of the work they describe, where they become not-themselves, or even become no-self, just an object to be encountered in space that resists temporal characterization. A pervasive loneliness in each piece gives way to the sense that the authors are writing from a timeless place where they are looked at but not able to be seen, and where remembered thoughts and feelings are reflections that ripple into the continuous present.

Though there are notable exceptions to every repetition, in most accounts you will find that the artist credited for the work is absent. Either they were never there or they departed as soon as the work was mounted. In their absence, and with the oft-described loose nature of the directions performers receive, many of the performers experience a tension over issues of ownership. While the artist designs the container, it would be void of content without the performer who makes a home inside of that container, drawing from past training and uncredited mentors. The performer is often a more visible author of the work than the artist, which is further amplified by the omnipresent mediation of smartphone cameras. In opposition to a darkened theater, where the social norm is that phones are put on silent and stowed at the start of a show, the gallery visitor trend is to document with abandon.

Holding up a phone screen offers a protective barrier for the viewer from the confrontational nature of live art. Unlike stationary art objects that wait, passively, to be witnessed, live works witness you back. The visitor's phone-in-hand can temper the anxiety of not knowing what will happen next in a performance, and as a bonus, offer evidence of having been there, physically present with the ephemeral. Selfies have become a fixture in the visitor experience. As effie describes, the more hours a performer experiences person after person transfixed by phone screens pointed at their body, the performer starts to wonder how far their image has spread; in what quantity of captures on how many clouds, and to what end. When the performer is naked, as can often be the case with performance gigs—in a medium where vulnerability is precious currency and shock-value might be the easiest path to notoriety, nudity is king—documentation becomes an even more sensitive topic. Paradoxically, sometimes the more exposed the performer's skin, the easier it is for them to hide behind the veil of their own objectification.

Another key difference between audiences in performance contexts versus galleries is that they can be heard. This is not only a question of increased proximity between performer and audience, but also a difference of design features. Without absorptive materials like curtains or cushioned seats, sound travels easily in airy and hard-surfaced gallery spaces, and so what is noticed and how meaning is made can be tracked in real time. Performers may overhear everything from theories about artist intention to analysis of the piece's success, and the questioning of whether a performance is improvised or set. Some receive shocked exclamations like, "It's alive!" I have occasionally heard gossip about the partners and coworkers of people I've never met, but think about days later with equal parts curiosity and guilt.

In addition to the auditory enhancement offered by gallery spaces, performance training teaches listening beyond the eardrums, through every fleshy surface and with every sensory cell. In hour three, when the focus really sets in, performers become bionic eavesdroppers. This is further heightened when visitors are not given a place to sit, or an explicit duration of a live work so that they can discern beginning, middle and end. Decisions about attention are made quickly and perceptibly. A performer's back can be turned to the gallery entrance, but they will feel people enter, pause for a moment, the brush of a quick gesture or vocal expression of disinterest, and the footsteps that fade away. Alternately, performers can hear statements of praise from strangers in galleries, which would otherwise come from friends and family, or those audience members bold enough to approach them in a post-show reception. The rare fit of applause echoing through a gallery hits differently than the obligatory clap when the curtain drops or the lights come up. Applause feels somehow personal and thrilling in its out-of-place-ness here.

Prior to March 2020, I did not hear any of my colleagues in the performance world debating whether or not they plan to keep taking this kind of art world gig work. Instead, I regularly heard some of the most incredibly talented dancers I knew talk about quitting dance entirely. Perhaps art world work is appealing to performers in its placid, almost-soothing nature because there is no room for growth in the gallery gig economy. There may be a sense of competition to get the job, and you may get more gig-work as your CV grows, but the work and its conditions remain more or less the same.

Undeniably, there is also a great deal of pleasure to be found in the work, despite the monotony of its production. There is a richness to the kind of intimate and messy relationships it forges between a performer and their audience, and a glamor to the cachet and intrigue that accompanies a big museum show.

Pleasure and glamor aside, yet another reason that dance and theater-trained performers are drawn to visual art gigs is that they need to work. And not just for financial reasons, albeit, that is an absolutely essential reason. There is a drive to work—and work *hard*—baked into performance training itself. For dancers, and in physical theater training as well, sweat, discomfort and pain are rewarded. They are well-recognized signposts on the long road toward technical goodness. To be good is to be within reaching distance of perfection, which is constantly described but cannot be demonstrated; just an impossibly bright horizon to look toward.

As a young ballet student, I was driven by a fusion of admiration and jealousy of the best dancers in class. I was taught to constantly compare my abilities to others as a necessary means of growth. More than competition with others, performance training emphasizes competition with oneself above all. Studios with mirrors encourage students' ability to transform their natural shape—a skill that is always in need of improvement. To be a trained performer is to know you can always do better. There is always more to give, more work to do, even when it means getting better at doing less. When learning something new, movements are big and effortful. The mark of a professional is the virtuosity of subtlety.

With the desire to perform and the desire to work hard intrinsically linked, visual art gigs lacking in instruction and feedback can feel dissatisfying. There is a tension in this particular field of labor which is recognizable in Kestrel's descriptions of frustration at not being able to use all of the muscles of her skill and Jessica's search for a performative foothold without any direction but to be still. With its often slow pace, limited directives, object-like physicality and extended duration, this kind of work often asks its performer to reckon with doing nothing, which can keep a performer endlessly engaged by its impossibility. The snake eats its tail and on we go; the meaningless meaning-chase may wear us out to the point of convincing ourselves we've found a meaningful challenge in it.

At the end of my day at the Walker, I am in front of a painting by Kerry James Marshall. A Black family lounging on a boat with a billowing sail portrays a serene reclamation of the shark-infested sea in Winslow Homer's harrowing *The Gulf Stream*. The glint of the water in Marshall's *Gulf Stream* is… beautiful. I hate the emptiness of that word, but sometimes it feels like the best container for the swell of sensations that encompass an aesthetic experience. I also know a painting isn't going to judge me for making a reductive or invasive word choice, even if I say it aloud. But I would never lean in to tell a performer they are beautiful at the moment it strikes me to be true. Maybe it's not fair for performers to compete with paintings in galleries when an art object's inhuman nature allows us to react with ecstasy or immediate disinterest without consent, guilt or shame. They make bearing witness comparatively effortless, while performers in visual art spaces are strangers. A performer's presence, and command of presence, can be a struggle to contend with, especially without practice. To encounter a performer where they are not expected might even elicit fear, as was the case for a colleague at a gig where multiple gallery visitors reported his "threatening behavior" to museum guards. The color of a performer's skin, their shape and size, and the gender they present contributes to visitors' perceptions of their interactions, significantly impacting the performer's safety no matter how mundane the work. The pandemic brought to the fore a reality already obvious to many: spaces populated by strangers feel tangibly charged with the myriad risks of lasting trauma.

As performance starts to occupy more of my life again—my lapse of faith, a memory, and the pandemic officially declared "over," three years later—I have been relearning what draws me to it. I remembered it as an escape from reality when the world was shut down. But performance is not only an enactment of world-building, it is a tool for world-seeing. As constructions, performances bare reflections of polylithic social realities that have been here all along. The practice of being an audience member cultivates a willingness to see the layered versions of one another not just for what we are and have been, but what we can and will be. As an audience, we bear witness to fellow humans at work; practicing presence, practicing asking to be seen. And in return, we practice being present with them. I wonder if audiences would grow if it were common knowledge that beyond the initial discomfort of watching people who know you're looking, live performance offers communion, and with it, a potent tool for endurance. Throughout 2020, I was constantly reminded that a sense of curiosity about and responsibility to strangers is the key to survival. This is not something I can unlearn, and I bring it with me in my work as a performer and audience member.

In its final, physical form, this book is a love letter to communities that keep showing up for one another, and keep valuing one another when others won't, or don't know how. More than an enumeration of some eccentricities of performance, it is human connection that makes up the binding material of this collection. My hope is that readers will feel welcome to stay with these stories and experience shades of self-recognition, even if they are unfamiliar with the artists or works described. Stripped of their context and conditions, many of the experiences and dynamics described here are not exclusive to performance. This occupational narrative project could be applied to an infinite number of fields. I would love to read those essays, I hope you will write them.

Lastly: I want to express my deep, whole-hearted gratitude to the artists who shared their stories here, to Matt from Insert Press, for believing this book needed to be published, and to Eileen, the illustrator with whom I've spent the last year constructing portals for readers to experience each essay in a way that refuses singularity. Thank you for giving me a reason to keep coming back to all of this, again and again.

Mireya Lucio

In October of 2011, with a fresh MFA in theater from CalArts, I was scrolling through my facebook feed at my corporate job and came across an audition notice for a Marina Abramović performance at the upcoming MOCA gala.

> Auditions Nov 7-9 for rehearsal & performance Nov 11-12 in downtown Los Angeles, conceived and directed by world renowned artist Marina Abramović.
>
> Seeking dynamic adult men and women, 5'-6' tall, with excellent physical stamina, focus and discipline. Long sustained stillness and silence involved. Limited speaking roles also being cast.
>
> Age and ethnicity open.
>
> Men need to be clean-shaven or have well-trimmed, minimal facial hair. No jewelry will be allowed day of performance. No facial tattoos, please.
>
> Mandatory rehearsal and performance dates: Fri. & Sat., Nov. 11th & 12th
>
> —Marina Abramović Auditions, October 26, 2011

I admired her body of work and, as I sat at my cubicle under harsh fluorescent lights, the idea of putting my mind and body through something challenging, durational and contained was very seductive. I sent an email with my height and performance experience/training, along with a photo of my face and a full body image (they specified no nudes).

I received an email saying I had been selected to audition for one of the six nude roles. At the audition at the MOCA Grand auditorium, Marina and her two assistants explained the concept: for a single night, performers would become centerpieces for the MOCA fundraising gala, making eye contact with guests, most as rotating heads in a loose adaptation of *The Artist is Present*, and six nudes reenacting *Nude with Skeleton*. We were told we would be there from before the guests entered until after they left, about three and a half hours, that the guests would be instructed not to communicate with us, and that we were to remain in the performance for its duration with no breaks. We would be paid $150 total (plus a one-year membership to MOCA) for one day of training and rehearsal, and one day of tech and performance. We took turns undressing and laying on tables with skeletons on top of us, six at a time, for what I guessed was about fifteen minutes. I was #5.

I received another email saying I was being cast as the seventh nude, the understudy. The next day (the night before the rehearsal) I was told I had been promoted and would be performing as one of the six nudes. The morning of the rehearsal, November 11th, a letter began circulating in which Yvonne Rainer was protesting the exploitation of the gala performers, both for the poor pay and for our potentially unsafe working conditions. Rainer had received an email from someone who had dropped out of the gala:

> *So, I spent an hour today at the Abromović [sic] audition at MOCA. The deal is that the artists/dancers she will hire will spend 3(!) hours under the dining tables of the donor gala with their heads protruding from the tables. They will be sitting on lazy susans under the table and slowly rotating and making eye contact with the donors/diners. Of course we were warned that we will not be able to leave to pee, etc. That the diners may try to feed us, give us drinks, fondle us under the table, etc but will be warned not to. Whatever happens, we are to remain in performance mode and unaffected. What the fuck?! And the chosen performers*

are expected to be there all day friday and saturday. The hours probably total 15 or more and the pay is $150 (plus a MOCA one year membership!!!). I am utterly appalled. This should be illegal. There is another audition for another role where the performers lie naked on tables with fake skeletons on them. Since I cannot stomach being a turning, severed head while people get drunk in front of me, I am seriously considering taking a naked role and performing an intervention at the gala celebration where I use my body as a surface to communicate the fact that I worked x number of hours for $150. I swear I need to do something... to speak for my community of artists who are being taken advantage of by major museums. sick shit. God, we need a revolution.

This is how I learned that I had replaced the whistleblower.

There were probably around one hundred people at the rehearsal, all wearing black turtlenecks and comfortable pants. Most of the performers were to be "rotating heads," about a dozen were cast as a "chorus" that would recite Abramović's *An Artist's Life Manifesto*, and seven "nudes."

The rehearsals:
time spent waiting, talking to people I knew, looking around at all the faces

o

feeling a tangible shift in the electricity in the room whenever Marina walked in, speculating about how cultivating presence for a lifetime might change the molecules in the air around you

o

the event planner, who talked and occupied space like a "Hollywood guy," changing the vibe

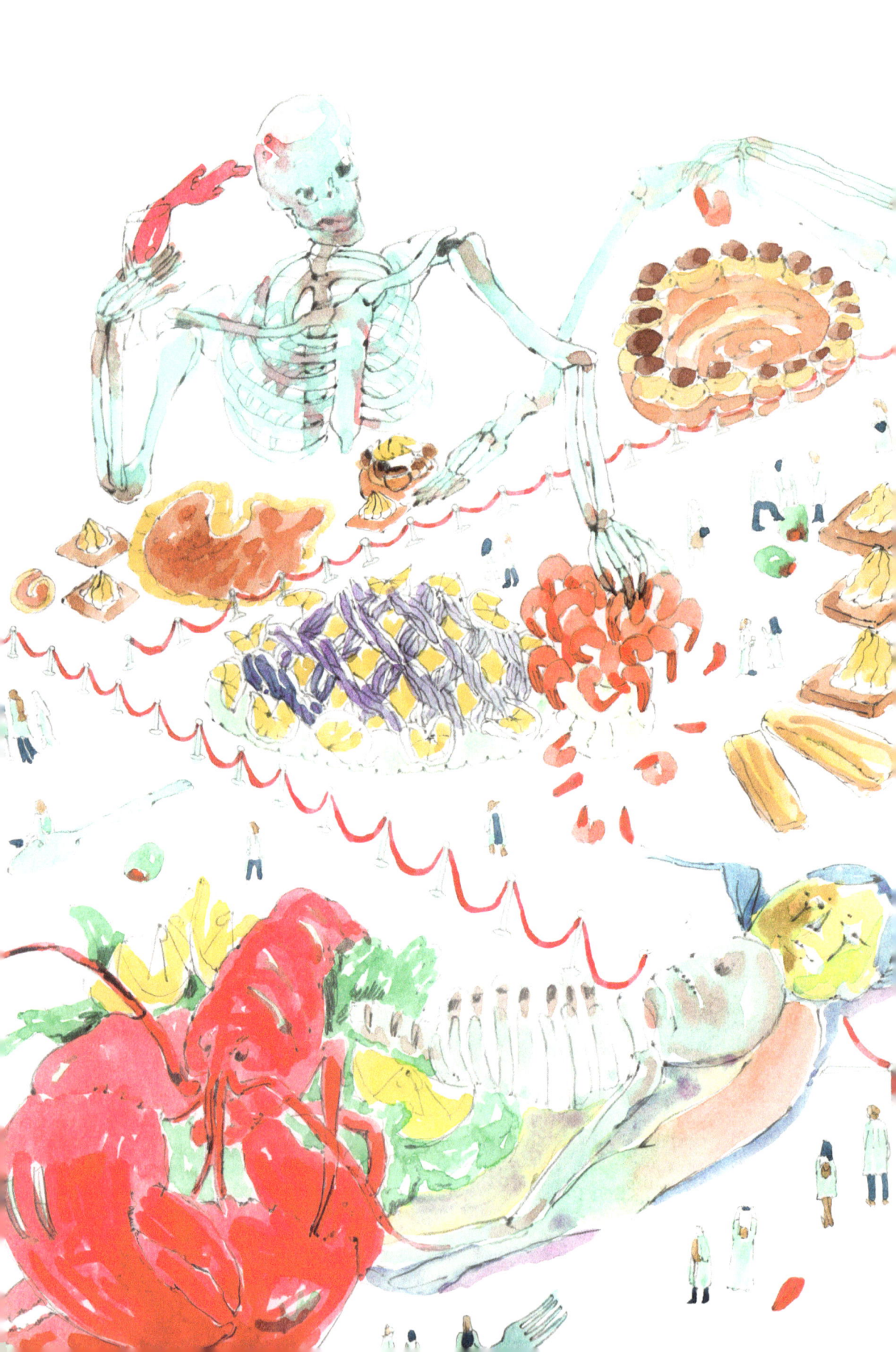

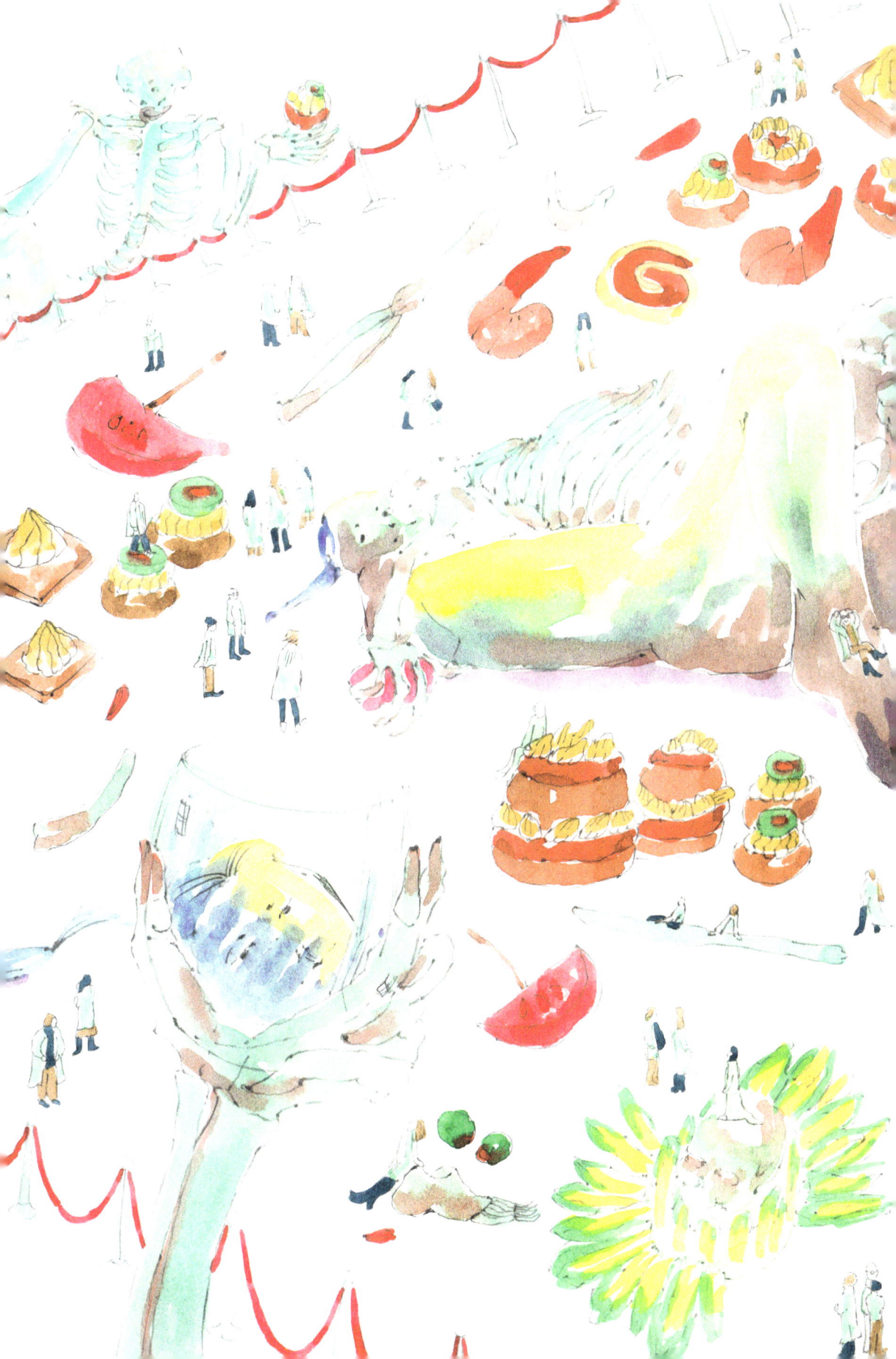

○

    Marina coming in in a flurry, hands at her heart, addressing us about her distress at Yvonne's letter; someone I knew reading a letter of rebuttal, some people clapping, a few others getting up to voice their concerns and wanting to start a dialogue about the situation, the event planner telling Marina she had to go, Marina saying she wanted to stay and be "with her artists," but leaving quickly after

○

    thinking I agreed with the criticism but that honestly I probably would have done it for free because I just wanted to know what it was like for my body and mind to go through something like that

○

    changing out of my clothes and into a robe, going outside to the tent where the gala would be held, sitting around the tables while event-dude explained what would happen, noticing that Yvonne Rainer was sitting among us, wearing a black turtleneck, asking people questions

○

    disrobing and getting on my table, the skeleton digging into my sternum, noticing that there was a round mirror in the ceiling over the table, seeing my reflection, being cold, wishing I had a stronger meditation practice, thinking it would be warmer once there were more bodies in the tent

○

    "...stay completely still... make eye contact as the table rotates... guests will be informed not to communicate with you... in case of emergency, lift your arm over your head and we will relieve you... guests will be wearing lab coats, which will shift the energy in the room and how they relate to you..."

trying to catch glimpses of the other nudes, finding comfort in witnessing them

The day of the performance we gathered in the auditorium. There were three people doing hair and makeup. Our hair was slicked back, tight against our heads, held in place by large amounts of hairspray. The three tattoos on my torso were covered up. There was a black plastic sheet on the floor of the stage and the nudes were asked to stand, naked, arms and legs outstretched, while they airbrushed us. The rest of the performers were sitting in the audience seats, facing us while checking their phones, talking, eating, and occasionally watching. There weren't enough roasted veggie sandwiches for the vegetarians.

As I waited for the announcement that it was time to go, I felt nervous and excited. I tried to quiet my mind and slow my breathing. I did some stretching. I peed. I looked at my reflection in the mirror and I caught other people's reflections. We all kind of looked the same: sleek, personality-less and glow-y.

We were walked to the tent. I walked to my table, #6. I handed Marina's assistant my robe. There were table settings now, except for two that had been removed for me to step through. I stepped on the chair, then the edge of the table. Crouching, I took a breath before stepping on the middle platform. I laid down, face up, feet hip distance apart, I shifted my buttocks so they were even under me, slid my shoulder blades back, shook my neck from side to side, finding space and length, rotated my ankles, felt all the points of connection with the surface. Breathed. The assistant carefully placed the skeleton on me, its head next to mine, its spine on a diagonal across my breast and sternum, its tailbone on my pelvic bone, knees on knees, feet in between my ankles. She opened the skeleton's arms to drape over mine, its hands inside of mine. She put her hand on my upper arm, and with a warm squeeze, whispered: "have fun." I heard her step off the table. Someone put the place settings back. The table center started turning. I looked at my reflection in the mirror, made eye contact with myself, acknowledged some vague starting point, and then turned my neck slightly to the right so I could look at the chairs. Someone announced that the guests were about to enter. I heard the flaps of the tent open and the distinct buzz of a crowd getting closer.

The performance:
People in fancy dress wearing lab coats. Phones up, taking photos, video.

o

The guests of table #6 start to find their places. No one I recognize. I hold eye contact for as long as I can before the table turns me away, then find someone else.

o

I'm not prepared for the phones. It's not that I'm being recorded, but that the guests have an object they can use to mediate the way they watch me. I have nothing to mediate my experience, except for the mercy of this table, turning me away.

o

Two women whisper to each other and giggle while looking at me. A man solemnly returns my eye contact.

o

There are appetizers on the table. Someone jokingly offers me food, a drink, a cigarette. People are eating, looking at me with various levels of discomfort, or ignoring me, turning to talk to someone behind them, then looking at me as if they had forgotten I was there, reaching for another piece of bread.

o

There are things that mark the passage of time. Opening remarks. A song performed by a professional mourner. A new course being served. And there are things that pull me towards an endless, timeless void: the outer corner of my right heel digging into the table, the spine of the skeleton wedged on my ribcage, a tear rolling out of the corner of my eye and pooling in my ear, my pelvic bone crushed by the weight of the skeleton's tailbone, my neck stiff under the weight of another head. Any adjustment must be made with imperceivable movements. I move parts of my body so slowly that they are not moving at all. One by one my ailments are addressed with microscopic shifts that feel like epic sagas unfolding.

o

Debbie Harry comes out. We must be close to dessert. Everyone on my table gets up to dance. I decide that I don't owe these empty chairs my eye contact. It takes me two entire songs to turn my head up to the ceiling. I catch my own reflection as *Heart of Glass* starts to play. I'm bathed in pulsing purple lights. There are half-eaten plates all around me. Immense loneliness floods my entire being. I am a centerpiece.

They didn't wait for the guests to leave. Sometime after the naked cake replicas of Marina and Debbie had been served, and the chorus completed their performance by spilling coffee from holey cups all over their lab coats, event-dude came to my table. He shook my arm and told me, "Ok, you're getting up." Time suddenly sped up. The skeleton was brusquely lifted from my body. He pulled me up to a seated position. My body was so stiff. He threw a robe on my shoulders, hurried me off the table, and with a firm grasp on my arm, began pulling me towards the exit. He said something about a round of applause to the onlookers. My legs were so heavy, everything was moving so fast, and I couldn't formulate words. I desperately wanted things to slow down. It took a lot of effort to put my arms through that robe. I was handed off to someone else, and was accompanied to the elevators.

After crying in the bathroom stall and putting my clothes on, my friend Chris and I stole some party favors and ate a slice of Debbie Harry's red velvet cake leg.

Casey Brown

I hope I'm not getting too sweaty. I just finished class at UCLA, and I'm walk-running on my way to perform Maria Hassabi's *PLASTIC* at the Hammer Museum. I stop by my apartment, gulp down a yogurt drink, and I'm off in my all-grey costume: a long-sleeved, collared shirt, the tightest jeggings I've ever owned, Keds, and a side braid to the right. Halfway there, I realize I forgot deodorant.

This is my first of two 2-hour shifts today. I had one yesterday and the day before that. A handful of local dancers and I take turns performing a looping sequence of poses, so there's always a performer while the museum is open, from 11am to 5pm.

Arriving at the museum, I make eyes with the desk then marvel, like always, at the entryway art. I make a mental note to visit museums more often.

I'm early, so I hide out in an upstairs conference room, counting down the minutes on my all-white watch. There, I run into one of Hassabi's company dancers. *PLASTIC* isn't Hassabi's only performance work at the Hammer. While *PLASTIC* continues on repeat in a small room, Maria and three company members also perform durational work in the museum's atrium. We talk slo-mo performance art as I stash my bags and then, boom. Time to begin.

I use the elevator to avoid a group of Hassabi's performers, whose bodies are sculpturally laid face-down on the stairs. Casual as a museum goer, I walk up to the door of what will be my room for the next two hours. I pretend to look curiously inside, but the door is opaque, so instead I spy on the visitors behind me. I quiet my heart rate, but my mind, hyped from my day, races on hyperspeed:

Are people stopping to look? If so, smile and shift weight. Am I too still—should I mix it up and move my hand? Ok good, no one's watching. Uh oh, she saw me looking at her reflection. Smile coyly then divert eyes!

On cue, the previous dancer in an identical costume walks out of the room and right by me, no look, no smile. After all, we are performers. We have business to do here.

Carefully, I pull the door open and enter what feels like a shrine.

It's all black in there: black carpet, black walls, a giant black beanbag chair, and a cluster of stage lights oscillating slowly between pitch-black and blindingly bright. I exhale. *Finally, I've arrived in my cocoon outside time.*

o

Throughout my shifts I was mostly bored. From beginning to end, I'd shift between about thirty different poses which I held between thirty seconds and two minutes. Hassabi facetiously called this her "amazing choreography"—sitting on the beanbag, standing, looking around, lounging, sitting, lying face-down, standing, out the door again. I had a simple job, and I did it well.

Bored was not bad. It was *almost* spiritual. Each performance was a new date with sensory deprivation. My heart rate dropped, I relaxed, ran out of thoughts, lost weight. At times, I'd get the floating-in-circles sensation that comes when you hold still for too long and your body loses the ability to remember its location. Walking after that was the hardest part, my sleepy limbs barely able to sense themselves, let alone amble in slow motion.

Doing nearly nothing took immense, constant concentration. The more I performed the score, the less I thought about it. I felt the "observer" part of me start to differentiate from my body. I became two: one of me was a body performing on autopilot; the other was free, deepening, aware. I was also constantly counting the seconds between movements, which the choreography required. I got so good at estimating seconds that I rarely checked my watch.

o

About a week into performing, I became aware that my experience in the work was in opposition to that of the viewers. My premeditated action, their surprise. My comfort, their unease. My control, their wide-eyed wonder. Sometimes, as I was moving glacially slow, I'd lift my head and lock eyes with a viewer who'd stare back like they'd just seen Mona Lisa cross the street.

Who, me? This? I'd think, basking in their interest. I felt valuable.

One Saturday, I performed among a crowd of rowdy kids. I felt charged with so many in the room. I felt stealthy. No one had realized I was performing. On cue, I dropped my head, started a slow melt down to the floor. Viewers shrieked and skittered. "She's been performing this whole time!" "How long has she been there?" I reveled in a sense of play.

Reactions weren't always drastic. Some never realized I was there at all. Often, viewers entered the room, grabbed a brochure, and left. Sometimes, viewers would have lengthy private conversations before realizing they weren't alone. "Oh my God!" Lying against the corner, face down to the carpet, was a woman (me), and was she alive?

As much as viewers recognized my subjectivity, they just as often treated me like an object. Once, a couple took pictures imitating my posture, right next to me, and posted them on Instagram. They spent more time looking at their phones than at me, or at the room. Silent and immobile, I felt consumed.

I got used to viewers discussing me in the third person, as if I couldn't hear. Some people would try to talk to me, and when I didn't answer, they'd tell their friend, "She can't talk." Others had already

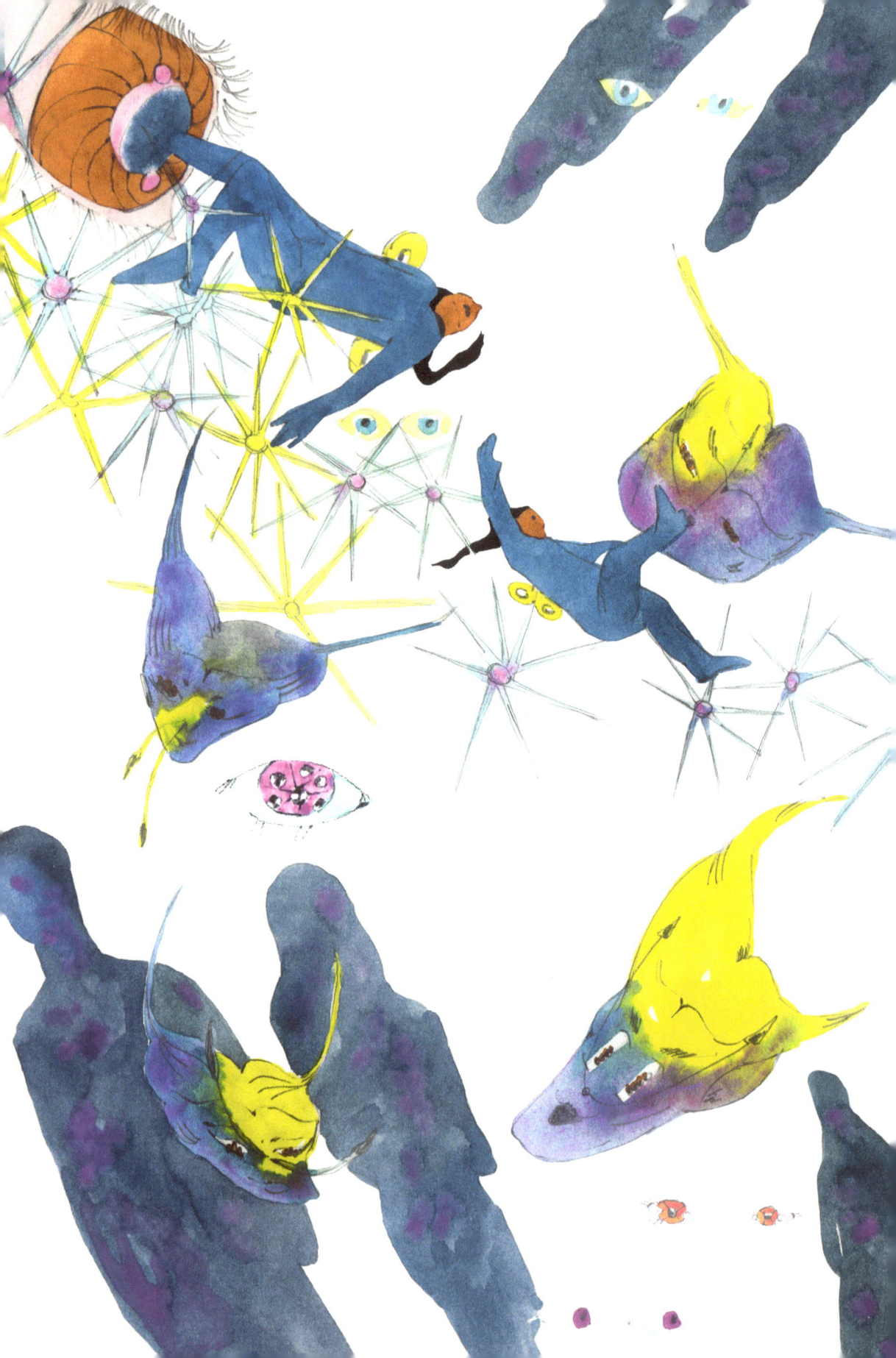

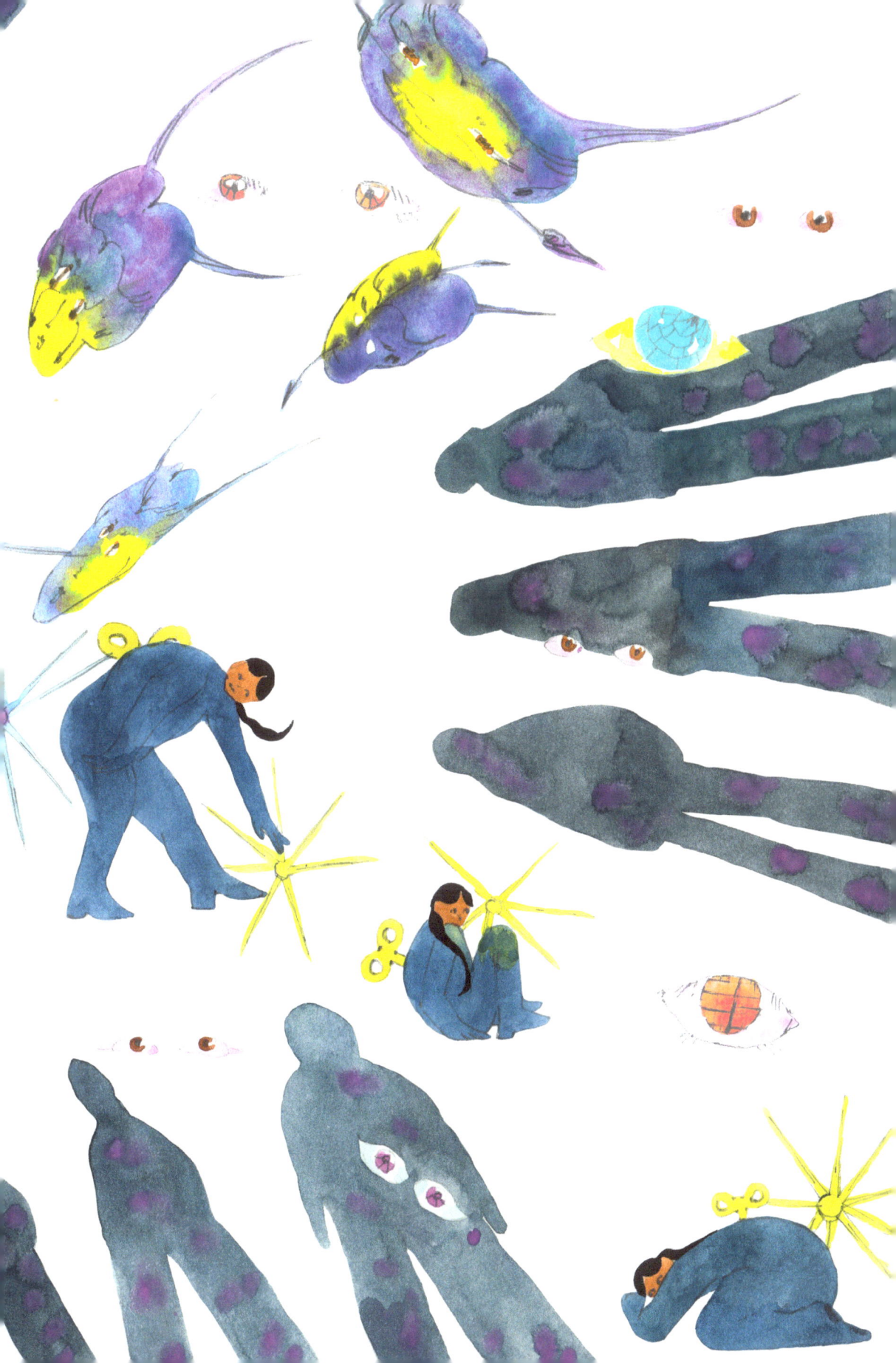

seen Hassabi and company doing similar choreography. They'd enter my room and say, "Let's go. This is just more of the same." Other times, someone would open the door, say, "Ugh," and leave. Very often, the door would open and close and no one would enter at all.

o

My biggest worry was that someone would stand in my way. We were instructed to say, "Please move," but I didn't want to speak. I didn't want to violate the choreography. I didn't want to disrupt my fantasy that nothing could stop the performance. I didn't want to see my silent power shattered in a breath.

We weren't told what to do if someone didn't move. In my final performance, a man sat in my way, blue eyes fixed on the lights. He was so stationary (intoxicated, perhaps), he performed objecthood better than I could.

I was only inches away when I spoke. "Please move."

No movement. My next move, if executed correctly, would put me lying on his lap. *Should I continue, right until we're skin to skin? Should I move a pace to the left, ruining my seamless flow? Should I run away?*

Luckily, Hassabi stepped in before I had to act. She whispered in his ear, and finally he moved. I was safe.

I should have been wary of sharing an opaque room with strangers and no guard, in a nearly public museum. My female body was hypervisible, but the deeper risk was my machine-like dedication to the choreography. This man could sabotage me as easily as sticking a hand in front of a wind-up toy, and I, the toy, would walk right into it. By this time, my experience of womanhood involved scanning for danger and then, when it appeared, improvising or fleeing. Why not here?

o

A minute into my first pose, gazing "into" the opaque doors I will soon enter, I hear a familiar throat-clear behind me. *Dad!* I told him to come straight to the Hammer Museum when he arrived from Florida, and here he was.

My skin prickles. Should I break from the performance? *Absolutely not*, I think. But the desire for action, a big hug, a smile, a wink, ripples through my body.

My inaction is conflicting with years of daughterly conditioning. When I was little, my dad, a pilot, would leave for days or weeks at a time. One time, he came home and I didn't get up. I just looked up from my book and said "Hey, Dad." He didn't let on, but he was devastated. Later, my mom laid down the rules.

"When dad gets home," she said, "you *must* hug him. Bare minimum."

At the museum, my father isn't upset, he's confused. I hear him pull out his phone and leave a voicemail.

"Hey Casey, it's Dad. I'm at the Hammer Museum, just wondering where you are. Anyway, if you get this, let me know where I should meet you." I can hear his all-cargo suit behind me crinkle as he paces: *Crswish, crswish!* It's deafening. I open the door and enter the room.

Twenty minutes pass. He enters, glances at my face, and leaves. *If only he paid more attention*, I think. I could take care of my father, even just wink his way, or I could perform the choreography without interruption. I keep my father in the dark and choose the choreography. I hate that.

A whole thirty minutes later, he blusters in again. This time, I look him in the eyes.

"Casey!"

Jessica Emmanuel

I didn't know much about the artist.

It was fine because it was simple. *I lay on this structure, they put clothes on top of me, and then I stay there for fifteen minutes.* No specific instructions were given for how to perform the piece, so I just had to rely on my common sense. This work was not a dance piece. It called for performers because people had to have the bodily intelligence to figure shit out on their own. They hired us to make it work.

There were two attendants to each structure, so each performer had two attendants who would help them come in and out of the structure and switch out with a new performer. If something was wrong; if we felt discomfort, if we were uncomfortable with people in the gallery or uncomfortable in the structure, if we were experiencing pain, or if anything was a red flag, there was a signal we could do with our hands to let them know, "I need out right now," and they would clear the room immediately and get us out of the structure to assist us with whatever we needed. I thought this was really considerate, and also imagined that something had happened to make it this way; that there was a time when people didn't have an out, or a way to tell anybody what was wrong.

There was a person who would check us in each day, to make sure we had arrived half an hour before our shift began. She wasn't called a stage manager, but that's what she did. She'd tell us when it was time to leave the green room and enter the gallery in our little booties, to make sure we weren't sullying the all-white space. The shifts were half-days, four hours at a time. We'd be on for fifteen minutes, with five minutes to reset and then fifteen minutes off. The scheduling became a problem when people were scheduled for times they weren't available, and so while I didn't have to, the performer in me had me doing back to back shifts so that the structure wouldn't sit empty. People would be late or not show up, so then they started scheduling alternates. Alternates were scheduled for whole shifts and would or would not perform depending on how the other performers' bodies felt.

Everybody laid on a structure on a raised platform, so we'd walk in our booties up to the platform and take a seat on our structure. Then the booties came off and I would slide myself into the pants and the gallery attendants would tie the shoes onto my feet. Once I was in the pants I couldn't really move, so I would sometimes get help sliding my arms into the hoodie. Then the gallery attendants would lay our hair so that it covered the poles. For some people they would put the hood up, because the pole stuck out through their hair. If the hair covered the poles well they got to leave the hood down, which would show more of a "floating" effect.

The thin structures supporting us were constructed out of poles. There were poles behind our legs, poles on our arms and a single pole along our backs. They looked like stick figures. Before the performances started we had a rehearsal day where all of the performers were invited to try laying on the structures, and for a few minutes it felt totally fine. Even in my first fifteen minute shift I was fine, but by the second one I felt a paradoxical combination of pain and numbness. My fingers started to twitch, other parts of my body started to move involuntarily. I didn't even know it was happening, until I heard voices say, "Look, she just twitched!" I don't know what this was, but I couldn't stop it. Part of the issue was that the structures were built for performers of different heights. Mine was for people five-foot-eight to five-foot-ten, but I found that two inches makes a big difference. I'm a long five-foot-ten, and the structure didn't reach my wrists, so I lost circulation in my hands.

All of the performers gradually accumulated cushions that they'd wear under the costume. Pads were made out of whatever we brought with us. I wrapped myself in anything I could find. We all brought more and more as time went by, eventually entering the gallery looking like football players. The position was so simple, but our discomfort was just due to overuse, I guess. I had one cushion under my head, one for my upper back and another for my lower back. I didn't ever have to strap my legs in, but I did end up strapping my arms to the poles. The straps were made from gauze that the gallery attendants provided. Actually, I did end up strapping my legs in because my hips would be in pain from holding my legs in position. It was just easier to strap everything where it needed to be. I learned over time that the more I strapped in, the less my muscles had to work. I found release through the restraints.

I wished that there was some kind of document from the previous performers of the piece, like an installation manual. I wanted to know how they found ways to sit comfortably, how they avoided cramping, and what they did when performers didn't show up. I thought that I wanted to hear from Xu Zhen, the artist who made the piece, until I found out he had never performed it. If he had, maybe the structures would have been made to comfortably support human bodies for extended periods.

Once I got fully strapped in, sometimes there would be a period of waiting for the other performers to get settled, and for the gallery attendants to wipe down the platforms. The gallery attendants would ask, multiple times, if everyone is sure they are ok. "You ready?" "You sure you're ok?" "Ready?". Then they would let the audience in.

The way that I was seated, in both positions I performed, I was looking straight up to the sky. I couldn't see anything else around me. I just had to shrug and tell myself: *Hope I'm safe. We're in a museum, so hopefully nothing crazy is going to happen.*

Tears came. Not emotional tears, but if you stare at one spot over a long period of time, and the air around you is dry, tears form. *I am laying back with my arms restrained and I cannot stop these tears from rolling down my face.*

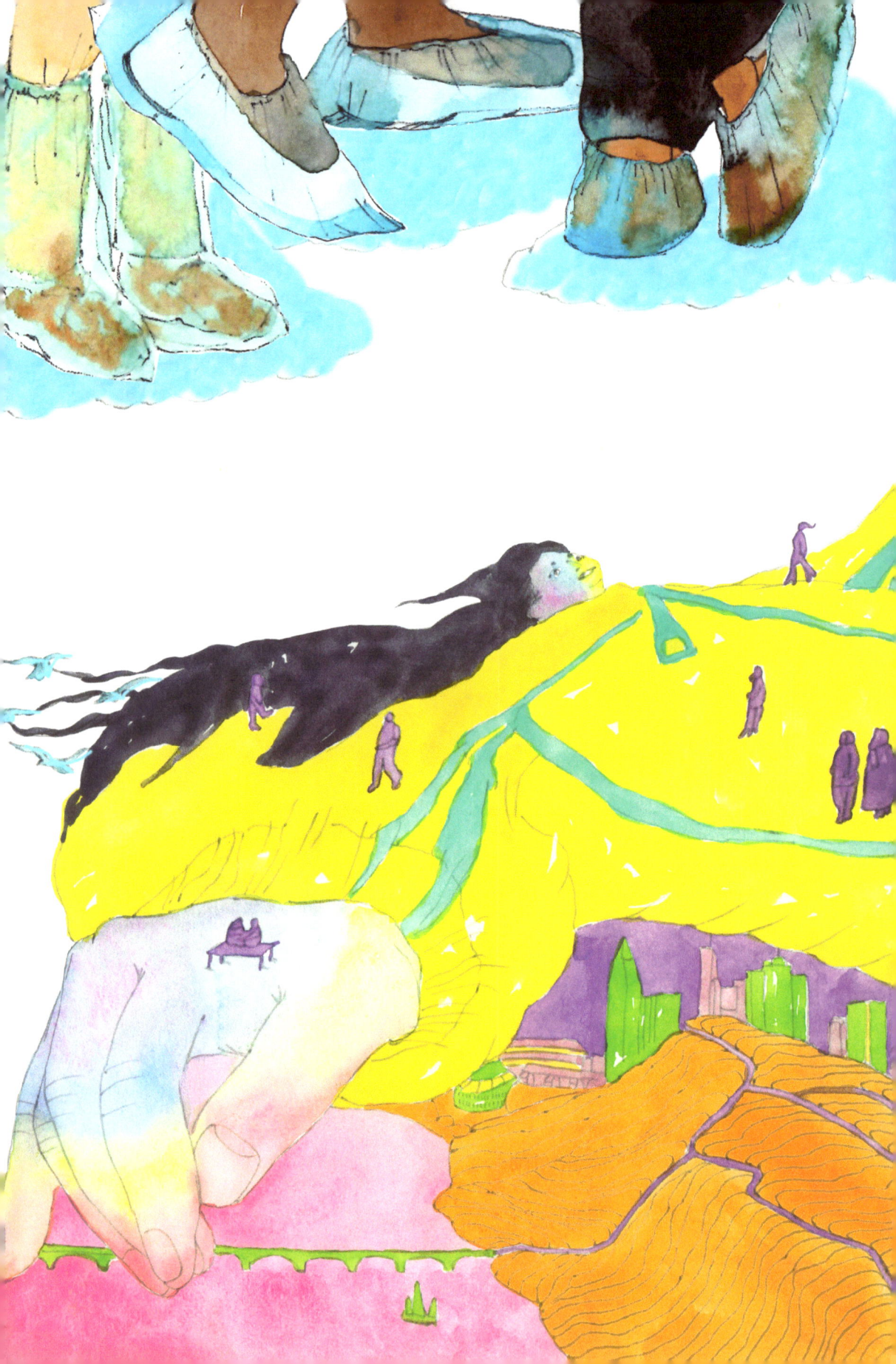

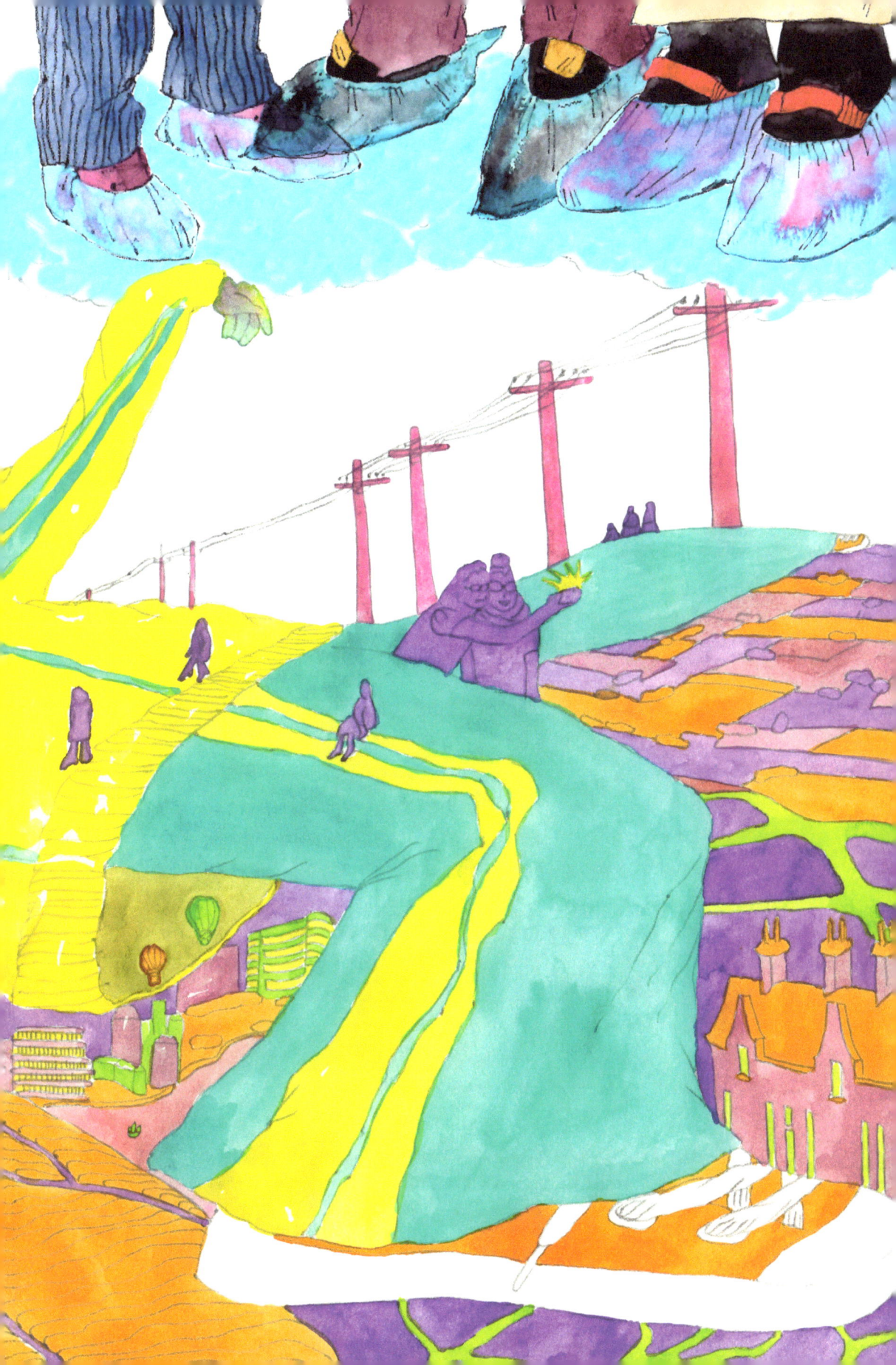

As the audience filled the space, at first I kept looking, looking, looking, without seeing anything. Then I turned inward. I tried to think about what I had learned in my research on the piece: Xu Zhen was exploring the precarity of Chinese labor conditions. I thought about migrant workers doing their best in a country where they don't have the rights of a citizen. They're leaving their home countries because the conditions were even worse there than living in a country where they don't have anything. I'd think about my own history with immigration. I'd think about my parents and what they went through to get what they thought would be a better life. I'd think about what it's like when things go wrong, but you don't have anyone to go to for defense, support, *anything*, because if anyone finds out that you're here you're at risk of deportation, and you have to keep working because you need to survive and there's nowhere else to go, so you have to withstand any and all abuse from the people around you. I'd think about the many ways in which abuse can show up when you don't have any support or protection at all.

After spending a lot of time with that, I started to meditate instead. I had gone to a dark place for a while and there was no one to guide me; no one to stop me from going too far. I realized that I didn't need to put myself through that, and I could make up my own shit instead. I'd meditate on work, creative pieces I wanted to develop, friendships and romantic relationships, how my body felt; I explored what it felt like to release into the structure and what it was to fight the structure and hold up my own weight. I explored letting my body be what it is, and what that was in contrast to trying to perform the work. I tried to say to the gallery visitors, *Look how fucking still I can be*. Sometimes I'd listen to what visitors were saying and try to respond with my body. Sometimes people would be endlessly going back and forth, "She's breathing!" "No, she's not breathing!" "She just breathed, though!" "I think she just blinked! "She might be a robot!" I tried to keep them guessing. They thought I was fake, I'd take a big breath, they thought I was alive, I wouldn't flinch. "Oh my god, she stopped blinking, but now she's crying!" I had to play these simple games for myself, because otherwise… otherwise, I was just staring at a ceiling for fifteen minutes—900 long seconds—freefalling. Alone.

My body gets tired when my mind isn't active. If I'm standing in a line, waiting for my order to be ready, I'll feel my legs tire quickly, but if I'm standing on a stage with a dramatic story grounding me from the roots of my feet, spiraling all the way up my spine and out through my gaze, I could stand there forever and it wouldn't feel like stillness. I want a "why." Why are we doing this? What does it mean? I want to perform why I am still. Am I sad? Am I scared? Am I so happy I can't believe it? Stillness can say a million things. I need some kind of purpose, or the boredom makes my body weak, and the weakness breeds pain.

I've been in other pieces, like Narcissister's work, where my whole naked body is exposed and there is no barrier between me and the viewers, but here, I was only a head and hands; sometimes hair. *They cannot approach me*; to protect the visual trickery, the platforms keep our visitors at a distance. *They cannot see me sweat, they cannot see the bottoms of my feet, they cannot see the history in my body.* As a group, the performers were not all women, not all femmes, not all one race, not all one size, and our identities were lost in the puzzle of how our bodies are appearing to defy physical laws. While I'm used to hearing the occasionally fucked up thing from a viewer about how they see me, in this work, positioned atop a large platform, balancing on poles, and buried underneath costumes and padding, I was shielded. Or at least they were not saying it loud enough for me to hear them.

Towards the end of the exhibition, I stopped performing entirely. I was just there. I had tried for a while, and I was glad to have tried. Then I accepted that nobody knows the difference. *They can't see what I'm trying to give them, and I don't even know if I'm supposed to be giving them anything at all. I'm not failing any instructions or disappointing any viewer in doing nothing. I am cushioned, I am laying down, and I do not feel guilty.* When I stopped performing, I started to work on myself. *Girl, you really need to meditate more.*

You know what you need to do when you get home? Yoga. Don't you need to pay off that credit card bill? At the end, it wasn't my piece and it didn't matter. *So let me make this about me: What do I need and what do I want?* Other performers started to fall asleep.

Finally it would be time to sweep the audience out of the gallery. That was the hard part. It was hard for the gallery attendants, but it was hard for us too. I could hear the attendants going through stages of asking people to leave. They would say that it's time to go, but that's when people wanted to stay the most, because that's when they wanted to take pictures. They were all waiting for everyone else to leave so that they could take *their* picture. We're done. We've done our fifteen, we're ready to go. The gallery attendants are trying to push people out, but they can't physically move them. They just have to keep trying to convince them to leave, and they're not going. That's just how audiences are. This is nothing new. They don't care. They're there for the spectacle of it, and to document that they were there, *at* the spectacle. The gallery assistants started telling them, "I understand that you think your picture is important, but you're putting the performers in danger by making them hold their positions longer than they are meant to." It was interesting to hear some people react with shock. They weren't thinking of us as human beings (human beings who might need a break). Other people conveyed that they didn't care, and continued to take pictures. One of my attendants started stepping into the frame of people's pictures. She would slowly walk toward them with her arms up, forcing them to back towards the exit. I found out at a bar after our last shift together that the attendants were all artists. It made sense then why they were so willing to help us.

After the last audience member finally left, the doors would close and a chorus of exhales would erupt in the gallery. "Oh shit!" "Get me out!" People would start tearing things off themselves if they could, and the attendants would quickly start wriggling us free. I was able to get myself loose enough to sit up on the structure on my own. Not everybody could, I was lucky.

We'd return to the green room and talk to the next group of performers about how it went. With the two casts of performers and alternates combined, there were at least fifteen of us back there. We'd share where we discovered we needed more cushion, and offer our cushions to one another for the next shift. We described micromovements that we experimented with to find incremental relief. We'd laugh about what we overheard: "I've seen this before, this is what street performers do." "Can't you tell? They're on wires!" "Oh! Their feet are glued to the ground!" Rather than wondering what the piece expressed, most people were trying to figure it out like some kind of math problem. We relayed stories about little kids behaving badly in the museum. One time a child climbed onto the platform and was trying to look underneath the backbending performer until they were removed from the gallery. Conversation would gradually shift to other projects we were each working on at the time. I loved hearing about other rehearsal processes, sharing takes on recent performances we had seen, what's happening with people's families and love lives, and learning about new body ointments people were using. We ate snacks, took Snapchats, stretched and laid on foam rollers. We gave each other massages and reiki. We had enough time. This was absolutely, *absolutely* the best part.

I've had a lot of people ask me about this piece. People that have never asked me about any other piece that I've done before; people that don't go see art, ever. Everyone wanted me to reveal how the magic trick works. I tried to make myself believe that it really was magic and I really was floating, but it wouldn't stick. It wasn't magic. Rarely do I feel magical when I'm in someone else's piece. No, I feel magic when I'm performing my own work. I may feel free, or I may feel something related to the ideas in the work. I may even feel like That Bitch, like, *yeeesssss*, like, in Narcissister's work, where I walked through a gallery naked and sat on a throne... but only when I'm saying what I want to say, do I feel like a whole-ass magician.

On my last day, all I remember thinking is, *who wants to get drinks?* I was taking so many gigs at that point, I didn't mourn the end of this show. I had a rehearsal for my next gig the following day. With gigs in galleries and museums, you never know when they'll decide to do an extension or bring the piece back, so there is no ending to the piece. It's just in storage. No need for goodbyes; we never knew the artist or anyone connected to the work, we weren't holding onto any stories, it was just another gig, done.

Kestrel Farin Leah

We entered the FIAC daily through its loading bay, along with the canvases, sculptures and construction materials. Inside, a maze of white temporary walls stretched as far as we could see in all directions, under the spectacular glass sky of the Grand Palais. Only Julien's booth would remain empty—it was the first time a Marcel Duchamp Prize nominee had presented a performance for consideration, and he had to endure a few rude comments over his "missing" paintings. I felt more fond of him for this—as a theater artist, I'm used to feeling like a bit of an outsider in the art world. We were permitted to caffeinate, change and warm up in the passage between press rooms, where I visibly exasperated the writers if I cautiously attempted a vocal warm up or rehearsed my French pronunciation. Quietly, maybe indignantly, the four of us shifted around each other on the little floor space we had, giving preference to the two that had real dancing to do that day.

I get a certain feeling right before I'm about to do any performance. It's the feeling of simultaneously having a great amount of power, and having none at all. I'm suddenly acutely aware that I could just *run* if I really wanted to—that I could abandon my post like a soldier deserting the troops—followed by the secondary thought that this is, well, unthinkable. It inevitably comes as I'm waiting to go onstage, and sometimes even in offstage moments during the course of a show. It's a strange thing—an inner rebellion against the fact that at this moment, my art becomes my duty. Instead of running, of course, I go on, but with a momentary sense of self-sacrifice. A slight variation of this conflict arises, however, when the performance I'm about to give actually feels like *work*. A bit of sadness sets in as I say, ok, I'll go on, but I won't give you all of me. I'll see if you notice.

As we descended into the exhibition space, I may have fantasized about making a sharp turn out the exit into the October air, but continued marching with my blue, American Apparel-ed clan to the nominee booths every forty-five minutes. All day we would walk the same path through thousands of spectators and purveyors, in the uncomfortable between-space that as a performer you just don't know what to do with—where surely no one can possibly be looking at you as *you*, but you're not yet performing. We lingered behind the crowd jammed against the mouth of the booth between us and our video-projected selves, until the projector went dark and we awkwardly nudged through the tightly packed bodies to take our places. A performance on repeat, just like performing for any extraordinary duration, is like endurance training. Once the first performance begins, the train has left the station and there's no way off. Starting felt like holding my breath before going underwater.

What Shall We Do Next? is Julien's archive, of sorts, of patented gestures for interfacing with new technologies, spanning smartphone technology, virtual reality and iconic scenes from Hollywood sci-fi movies, among other sources. From his research, he had lifted a series of hand gestures presented as the video animation *What Shall We Do Next? Sequence #1*. Then in 2013, in Los Angeles, he enlisted six performers, including myself, and a choreographer, to create a "choreographic abstraction" of patented movements. The work was presented as a live performance at Fahrenheit, Los Angeles, and then filmed to create the video *Sequence #2*. Four of us joined Julien in Paris for the FIAC that year, and upon arriving, built the performance that accompanied the video's exhibition. I don't doubt I landed the job in the first place due to some years of non-western theater training that helped me move very slowly and precisely, and, as the only theater performer and French speaker, I carried most of the text. It was no matter to Julien that I wasn't qualified to perform a brief burst of Martha Graham choreography that broke from our otherwise mechanical sequences of gestures, though it mattered quite a bit to me. That was, of course, until I realized without a doubt that it also didn't matter to the audience.

The video and performance were variations on the same theme: essentialized enactments of the (mostly hand) gestures and physical postures dictated by familiar devices or more novel innovations—flatly narrated with patent texts or factual explanations, and threaded together in a pretty tight choreographic structure. With blank faces and wooden lower bodies, we dragged and dropped on mimed interfaces, monitored imaginary Apple watches, or darted our eyeballs around as if reading with Google glasses, milling about the empty space as if in a personal void. Each action, plucked from its context, was isolated to the obscurity of *slowly spreads fingers / extends arm and forms fingers into a blade / shifts gaze rapidly right and left* ... We did most of this in silence, accompanied only by the occasional squeaking of our sneakers against the concrete, and the muffled clanging of what sounded like a catering crew somewhere not far from the booth. Piling mundanity on top of mundanity, I provided show-and-tell commentary as the others re-enacted the swiping, pointing and clicking performances of actors in sci-fi movies and their green-screened interfaces. We tied up the performance with the unexpected whole-body physicality of some truncated Graham choreography—perfunctorily demonstrated as two of us orated a bilingual summary of the choreographer's heir's legal battle to hold onto the rights to her work, showing that Graham, too, could be rendered utterly mundane. The video's narration had landed its final note on the alarming physical cost of excessively repetitive hand gestures, but (repetition giving way to variation in our performance) anyone paying attention might have been far more concerned by the combination of Graham with a concrete floor.

That cubicle—its concrete floor and four white temporary walls—was too small for our choreography. Likewise, everything about me—what I sense I'm giving off as a performer—immediately felt too big for its confines. I've come to understand that I'm in search of extremes—extreme transgression, extreme transformation. Even if

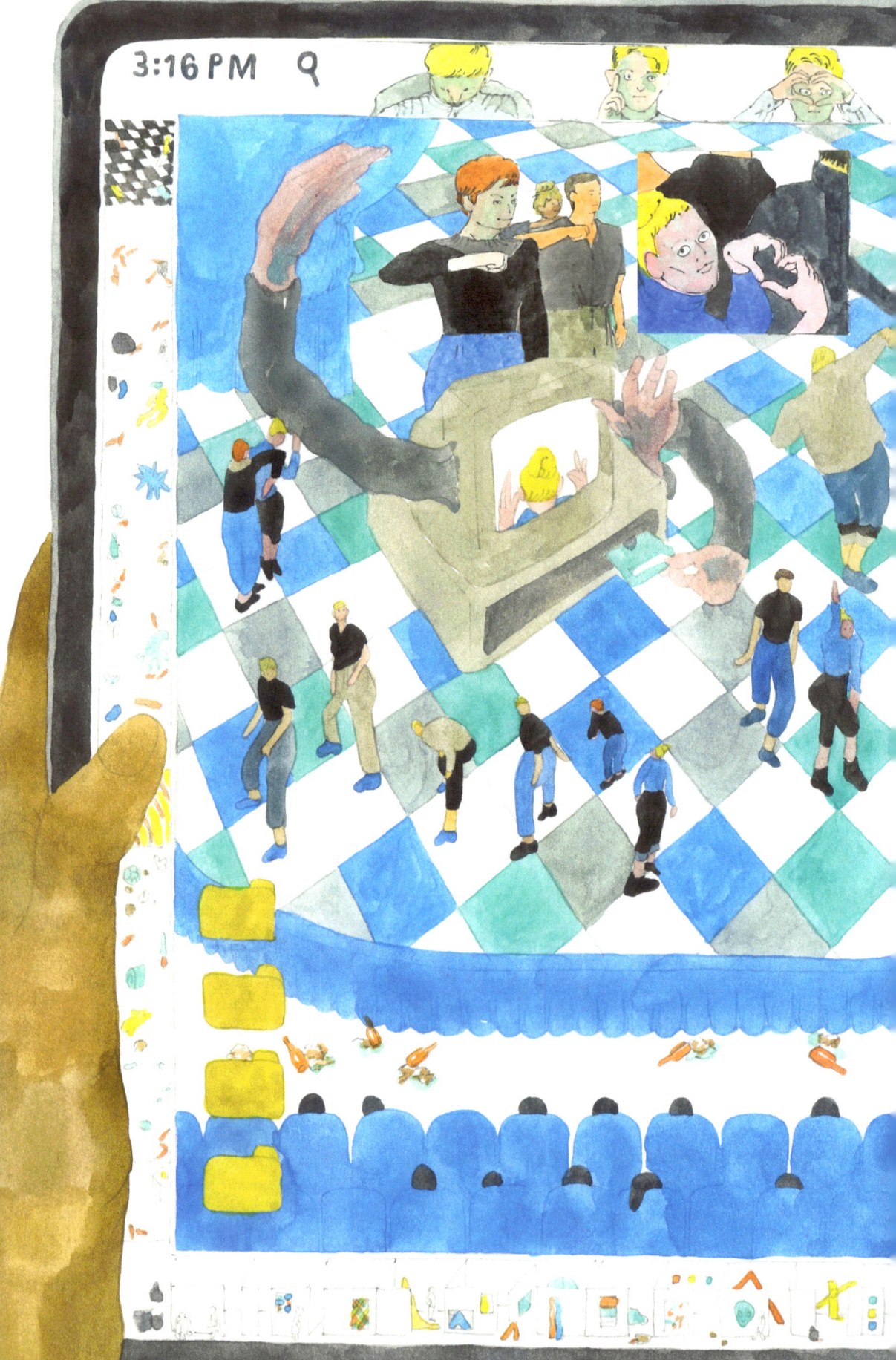

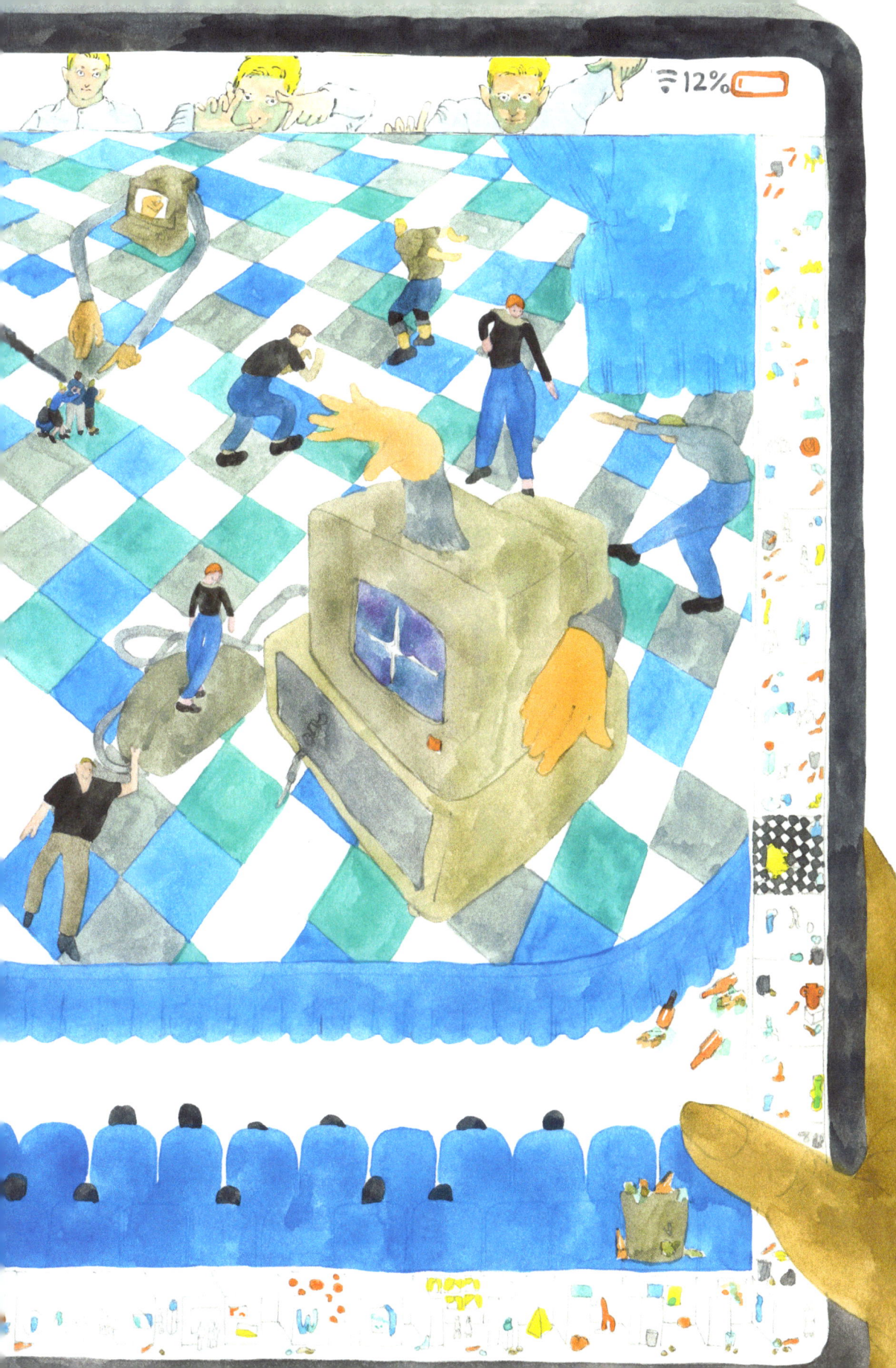

the material and scenario don't support the provocation I crave, I've started to feel that any act of performing thins the veil between the audience and my madness. The more people that crammed themselves in to create a human wall a couple of feet from my face, the more they edged us back in a way that might fuck with the blocking, the more monstrous I felt. Thank goodness, I wasn't supposed to use our proximity to create intimacy, and I wasn't supposed to make eye contact. I wasn't supposed to be addressing them, and I wasn't supposed to be myself. I never knew how to be myself in front of an audience anyway. I looked for the empty spaces between bodies to focus on, and inwardly cursed anyone who unknowingly shifted into my direct view.

I was happy to be in that booth. *I love touring*. I love waking up in another city and going all-in on my work because I'm far beyond the grip of any other responsibilities. And as far as this chapter of my performance work, it's an unfailingly alluring prospect: to try and unravel an artist's concept through my process as a performer, which is how I understand most things best. But after the usual satisfaction of "figuring out" the performance—its sequences and transitions, timing, rhythm and spatial relationships—it's not surprising that performing design patents all day quickly felt like *work*, not least because of the particular formality and fixedness necessitated by our performance being *for sale*. In theater, strict forms are only compelling if they contain a rebellion against them; that is, if they are in tension with the performer's capacity for abandon. The mechanical process being asked of me had the opposite, castrating effect of allowing me to be deathly passive.

When you're passive in a performance, it's easy to notice that your feet are hot; to remember that your jeans are tight in the wrong places, and to wonder if the size of your hips are under scrutiny; to notice that your eyeballs ache. You don't walk away feeling like you've done anything particularly important, and you don't seriously contemplate what kind of experience the audience had—surely that requires, at the very least, feeling complicit in the work's concept, or, in theatrical terms, its dramaturgy. But the strange thing is that while it was the performers who gave shape to *WSWDN?*'s realization as a performance, its concept never felt permeated by us, never felt in dynamic conversation with what might be discovered through the interpretation of bodies in space. In a performance so theoretically concerned with the body, mine felt the numb heaviness of being an untapped well—a feeling I tried not to add up at the end of each day. At this point, my role, as I saw it, was to make sure my execution was as flawless as I could humanly manage. It was a task I was trained for, but all it did was leave me time to think.

I was very aware that our performance was dominating the surrounding sonic (and energetic) space, and possibly distracting and drawing audiences from the other three nominee booths. Was it fair that the competing paintings and sculptures neighboring us were accompanied by a soundtrack imposed by us? After the first day of the fair, Julien's gallerist held a celebratory dinner in honor of his expected triumph where a guest gushed to me repeatedly, "Mais, *la performance!*" Her unbridled enthusiasm for our undistinguished performances made me deeply consider the attention that performing artists *demand* and whether we belong alongside other kinds of art work at all. Meanwhile, Julien's assistant was insisting that our first day was somewhat of a disappointment because I had dropped a line. With a head full of wine I tried to explain what it actually is to perform, and that performers are not objects and never will—nor should—satisfy a need for perfection. Two days later, my fellow performer and beloved tour buddy showed up with no voice, having left it in an after-hours nightclub.

The atmosphere in the press hallway changed distinctly after the first day of the fair and word spread of *"...la performance!"* Suddenly, stone-faced writers were smiling as they passed and even stopped to invite us to a party or two. Needless to say, it was a much more pleasant resting spot to sip on the free espresso we got from one of those detestable companies that sell disposable pod-eating espresso machines. I tried to make the most of our short breaks and wander the booths, but the density of artworks was cognitively overwhelming. After about five minutes, images began to blend together and started to have equal value, a lot like shopping at a high street clothing store. Anyway, there wasn't time to change out of costume and I didn't like the possibility of being recognized, like a piece of an artwork that ran away or got lost (the between-space). Not to mention, I felt dirty. After the press hallway began smelling of stale sweat, we finally begged for our costumes to be washed. According to Julien's program notes: *Away from the stand, the dancers also move about the corridors of the FIAC, making gestures which will soon be common in the art world, like a troubling anticipation.* Well, not that we were aware of, anyway.

Julien won the Marcel Duchamp Prize and our performance was promptly sold, while all of us wondered what exactly had been for sale. Julien himself didn't seem to know either—after the sale we talked about some kind of score or script that needed to be generated, each of us suggesting one way or another to notate what we had made, but it was never brought up again. We would go on to repeat the performance at the Pompidou's opening in Malaga, Spain, and at the Palais de Tokyo's DO DISTURB Festival, where artist Adam Linder (who was presenting his *Chorégraphic service n°1 : Some cleaning*) chatted to me about performance as labor over the hotel breakfast buffet. There was talk of further touring together, but after DO DISTURB, Julien replaced all of us with different performers.

Since then, I can't say I've thought much about the proprietary movements my hands are doing when I'm fiddling with my iPhone. But I have thought a lot about how credit and ownership were attributed in the performance we had created. It became more and more troubling to me that a project interrogating the domain of patent law over human gestures simply fell in line with the prescribed art market protocol of attributing genius to the singular artist as originator of the work. But it was an irony that was thoroughly lost on Julien, who seemed unable to consider our own process within his field of interest, even when I told him I was writing about it (see *Harvesting Theater*, The Theatre Times, August 2017).

> *Who, specifically, owns the gestures?*
> *(Mais qui possèdent ces gestes?)*
>
> *The dance companies?*
> *(Les compagnies de danse?)*
>
> *Their boards of directors?*
> *(Leurs conseils d'administration?)*
>
> *The commissioners?*
> *(Les commanditaires?)*
>
> *Do the choreographers themselves own any of the work?*
> *(Est-ce que les chorégraphes possèdent tout ou partie de leur travail?)*

What Shall We Do Next?, FIAC, 2013
Performed by Jos McKain and Kestrel Farin Leah

The closing day of the fair, we exited through the main space with the public, tipsy on champagne. We were allowed to keep our costumes.

Allie Hankins

Gordon Hall's exhibit *THROUGH and THROUGH and THROUGH* was presented by PICA in the summer of 2019. It consisted of eighteen sculptures that were accompanied by eighteen performance scores, with each score assigned to a specific sculpture. Each performer had three two-hour performance shifts, with a total of thirty minutes max of performing time. Performance scores lasted anywhere from two to five minutes, with the exception of one, which was thirty minutes. Performances were to happen in the space every twenty minutes during gallery hours, and unless multiple people were doing the same or a shared score, only one performance could be happening at a time. Gordon's intention was to have the performances occur with or without human audiences (the sculptures being audience as well). He believed that whether or not they were observed, the performances would activate the space, leaving an energetic residue that would be felt by gallery-goers.

On our one and only day of rehearsal, Gordon walked us around the gallery, sweetly introducing us to each of his eighteen sculptures and demonstrating their accompanying performance scores. He went in reverse order, so the first one we met was *Floor Door (For Freds)*. *Floor Door* is an outline of a door (complete with handle) made of paper, colored in with colored pencil. It is delicate and unassuming, but the performance score that accompanies it is one of the most bombastic:

> *One person in a car drives up and parks, or double parks, in front of the exhibition. Windows rolled down, they play a song on the car stereo, in its entirety, as loud as possible, with silence before and after. Song selection is open, but must be popular music from the last thirty years and recognizable to most. They drive away when [the] song is over and don't come inside*

or announce this in any way. The volume should be such that a person in the gallery can hear it only faintly in the background.

I was struck by how the performance score tethered the sculpture to the soundscape of the world outside. It's not that I felt like his sculptures were in any way incomplete when their performance counterpart wasn't being performed, but I got a warm feeling imagining that this door was always awaiting that blaring music to illuminate the additional dimension of itself. I never got to execute that performance score because I didn't have a car at the time, but during the run of performances, I fantasized about a sudden sonic interruption of Sam Smith or Selena Gomez or Ariana Grande as I performed one of the seventeen other scores so that I could have a tiny duet with *Floor Door*—a duet wherein I tried not to let on that I wanted to dance or sing along, and *Floor Door* basked in the warm vibrations of the sonic spotlight.

> **Brick Found with Kristan (found brick):** *Between one and four people do the "top-loading washing machine dance" anywhere in the space for as long as is comfortable, with arms hanging below the elbows, loose and flapping as they rotate back and forth. Starting and stopping is staggered within the group. Duration: Until it's unpleasant—2 min?*

In preparation to perform this score, I would often imagine a brick inside a washing machine. I would visualize it being tossed around, knocking into and damaging the central agitator, wreaking havoc inside the machine. I knew that in reality, the brick would probably sit sunk at the bottom of the drum of the machine, totally unmoved by the cycles, but at least it would come out cleaner than it was when it went in. The brick that Gordon included in the show was an example of an object whose sculpture-ness was manifest by the story of its discovery. Kristan (Kennedy, co-Artistic Director of PICA) saw it over a fence, it was retrieved, brought home, it provided inspiration, and it became the result in and of itself. As I performed the score, I would amuse myself by assuming the personality of the brick and think to myself, "Moments ago I was resting in the sunshine in a quiet field, and now I'm drowning." Some days I could relate to this sentiment even as a human. Gordon described the "top-loading washing machine dance" as "found movement," and it was particularly delightful to perform because of its borderline goofiness. Done for too short of a time, and it would risk feeling flippant or dismissable as wacky. But when done for long enough—especially when done by multiple people at once—the sound of the loose limbs hitting torsos, the surprising difficulty and mild discomfort in repeating the action would give way to an awkward serenity.

On that one and only rehearsal day, Gordon demonstrated all of the scores to us before we were asked to try them ourselves. They seemed so OF HIM, and so OF THE SCULPTURES at the same time. He became one of them—he already had an elevated status of being the person who knows more about them than anyone else—but seeing him do the scores that he dedicated to them opened up this other realm of life that the inanimate objects could be having. The scores that accompanied the sculptures were brief, many only two to three minutes long. It was the brevity that allowed a sudden burst of delightful inefficiency or awkward attempt to establish an intimacy with objects. Because I rarely had a human audience, the private nature of this performance experience sometimes led me to believe that I had a special bond with the sculptures and that perhaps my presence was soothing or even exciting to them. Over the course of the show, I attempted assimilation with the sculptures. I tried to communicate on their behalf or express something that they could not. I would imagine myself inside their thought bubbles. Over and over again, I was struck by how messy my humanness and all of my existential questioning was in comparison to the orderly placidity and assured nature of the sculptures.

The score for / \ can only be done in duet with another human performer, and the postures we assume closely resemble the shape the sculpture itself suggests.

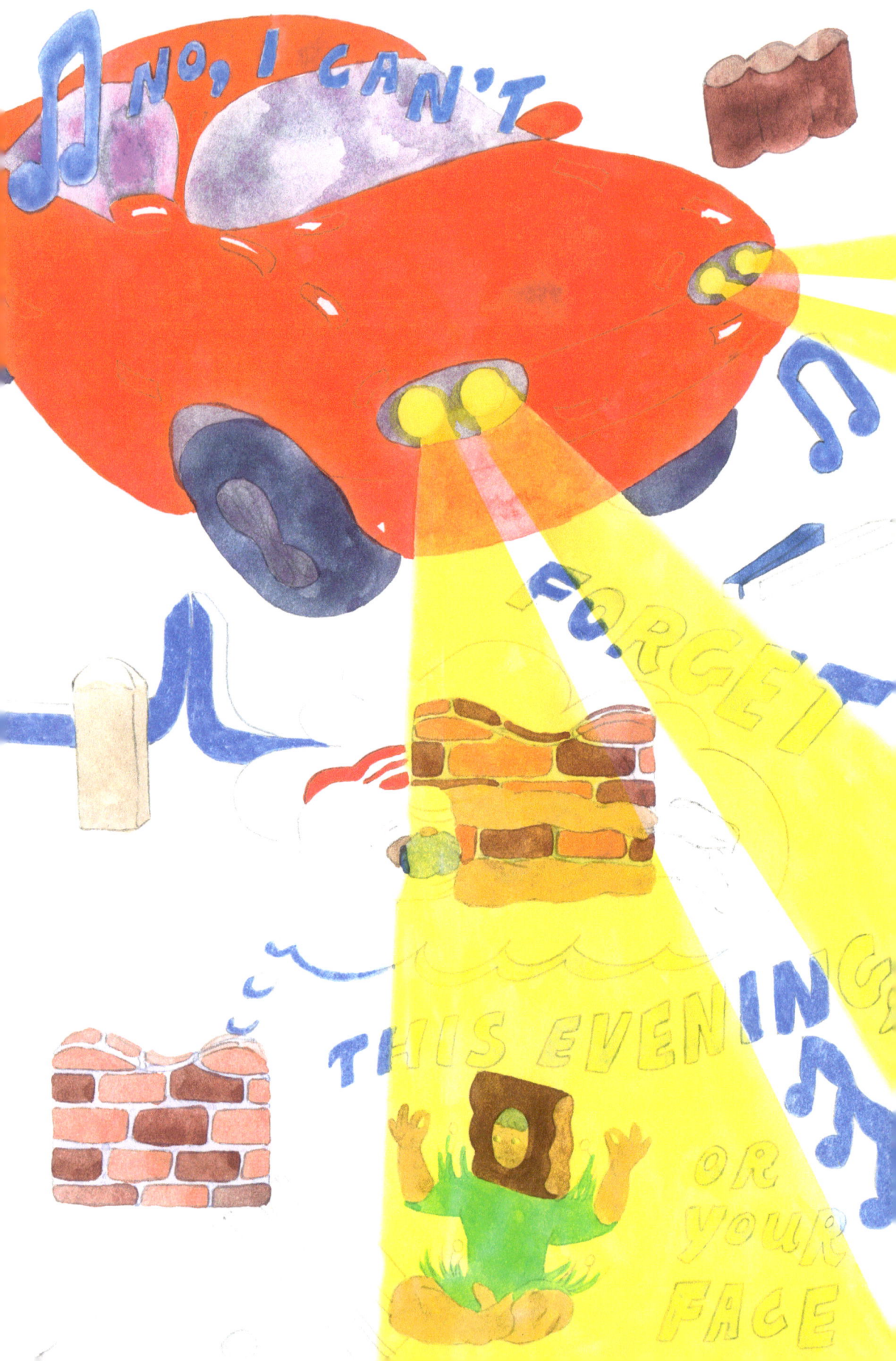

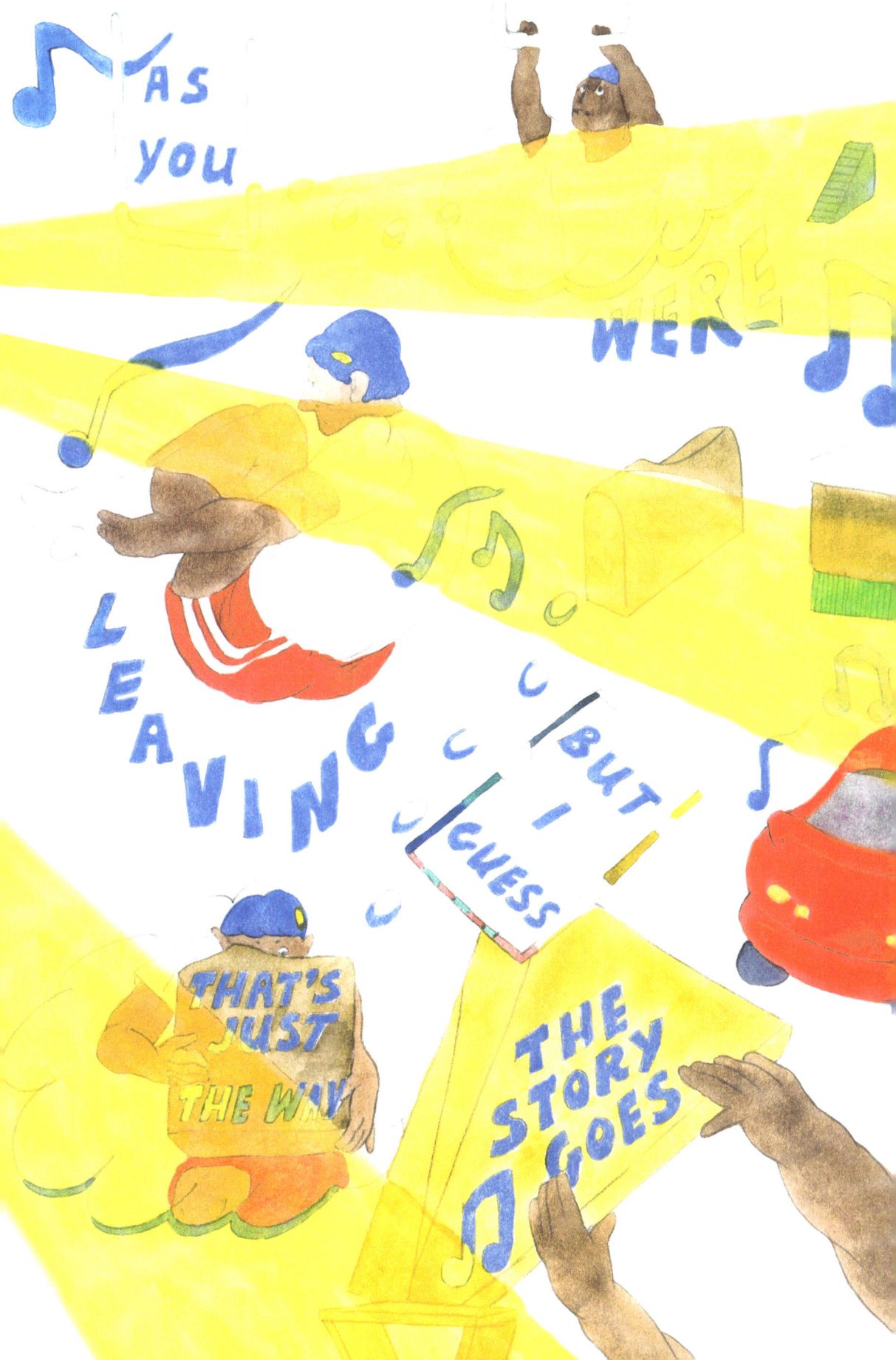

> / \ (colored pencil on poplar): *Two people stand on opposite sides of the gallery toward the back wall, clapping back and forth: CLAP / CLAP / CLAP / CLAP / CLAP/ CLAP Then yelling back and forth: WHO / DO / YOU / THINK / YOU / ARE? They yell loudly, and listen for the echo, playing tennis with the sound waves filling the long space between them.*

The day I perform this score, Linda and I agree to perform it together. We open the green room door and walk to our positions in the gallery. I take care to notice the distance between my body and Linda's, and I take note of the distance between my body and the sculpture whose score we are performing. I briefly consider scale; the smallness of the sculpture relative to me, the smallness of Linda and I relative to the gallery space, the loudness of our yelling voices relative to the persistent quiet of this gallery space. After Linda and I are settled, we punctuate the space with our voices as if speaking on the sculpture's behalf.

WHO DO YOU THINK YOU ARE? It was an indignant question that led me to philosophical consideration. Who DO I think I am? I knew it was impossible to ever see myself as others see me. I held an image of myself out before me. *THIS IS WHO I THINK I AM.* I understood I could never fully meet or become that person. The two slashes of / \ were angled toward one another—almost antagonistic. Their positioning mimicked the volleying of the words (or, I should say, the volleying of the words mimicked their positioning). In asking *WHO DO YOU THINK YOU ARE?* We were also saying *I CAN NEVER FULLY KNOW YOU. THERE WILL ALWAYS BE A GAP BETWEEN US. EVEN WHEN WE KISS WE ARE MERELY KNOCKING OUR SPACE HELMETS TOGETHER.*

I was one of the performers on the last day of the exhibition, and for the very first time, there were people watching me. Lots of them. There were also cameras, because Gordon needed documentation of some of the performance scores. Over the course of the exhibition, we had been advised to select a small handful of scores to cycle through during our performances. I was asked by Gordon via Erin Merrill, the gallery manager, to do several scores that had not been in my rotation. I rehearsed the requested scores in the green room, including *Carved Drawing*.

> **Carved Drawing (colored pencil on carved balsa wood):** *One person walks "with purpose" across the space from one wall of the gallery to the other, leaning down and flipping over Carved Drawing in the direction of their motion with two index fingers on each end, letting it rotate over on its corner without leaving the floor. Movement is quick, smooth, and performed with efficiency. This flipping over causes Carved Drawing to travel back and forth across the gallery, throughout the run of the exhibition, with alternate sides facing up.*

As I prepared to begin my walk across the gallery from one wall to the other, I looked at the camera set up directly across the space from me, at the opposite side of the gallery—the end of my pathway. As directed by the score, I walked with purpose from one side of the room, my index fingers extending in preparation. I briefly felt the pads of my fingers against the wood, and I heard the soft sound of balsa wood hit the concrete as I left it behind and continued my walk across the rest of the length of the room towards where the camera was standing. If that camera had been a human, I would have let myself see their face, acknowledge them in the space, not in any forced way. The glance or the interaction would have been fleeting, and just a consequence of two bodies being in the same place at the same time. But with the camera in its fixed place, waiting for me and recording in order to capture this ephemeral moment, I worried that this one fleeting action would become a *fixed* moment; a part of the score; a directive, which it wasn't meant to be. I was disoriented by the camera eye's ability to create a sense of permanence. I faltered. My gaze bounced to and away from the lens, and I veered left to avoid collision. I thought about that noncommittal glance for days afterward. I wondered, *Will Gordon think I made a weird face?*

One night, after the exhibition had ended, I was lying in bed in the flickering glow of the electric tea lights that my mother sent me for Hanukkah some years ago, and a pickup truck outside my house was playing Harry Nilsson's *Without You* on repeat. The volume oscillated between muffled and thundering, but even at its most quiet, the steady piano chords and desperate voice were clearly audible. As my gaze fell on the silhouette of a bouquet of flowers on my desk, I was reminded of Gordon's *Floor Door (For Freds)*. Suddenly it seemed possible that these two entities, the silhouette and the song, completed one another, and I laughed at the romanticism of it all. Now I'm imagining *Floor Door (For Freds)* carefully folded up and stored in some climate controlled space in NY, and I hope that it gets to hear some music from time to time.

effie bowen

I arrive ten minutes early, ushered to work by a prepaid car service. I enter the gallery before it opens, before some staff have arrived and definitely before any visitors have come. Per instructions from the artist I wear loose fitting clothes, and since my head is shaved, there's no hair I need to wrangle or braid. I carry a meal, a snack and a gallon of water for the day. It's morning and I'll be here past sunset. Glass garage doors and skylights fill the white-walled room with light. The floor is smooth, cold cement.

I share the space with only a handful of other staff but there is already an illusion that the room is scattered with people. Every artwork here is human-sized or person-like, providing a ghostly aura. A show of figures, some so hauntingly realistic, I turn around expecting a live person to be standing beside me. I am here to activate the only figurative sculpture in the show utilizing live bodies. I am here as a performer, a body, a disguise.

I walk behind the back wall into an office-turned-dressing room where there is a kitchen equipped with a stash of sparkling water and a coffee maker, a single-stall bathroom with a bidet, and a computer monitor flashing live images from the security cameras. I put my lunch in the fridge and drape my jacket over a swiveling office chair. There is no doubt that this space usually operates as a meeting place, our privacy in this ad hoc dressing room is completely subject to spontaneous conferences between curators, assistants, and staff. On rare occasions between shifts, we are forbidden access to our dressing room due to highly private meetings with collectors.

We are independent contractors and at the utter whim of the needs and mayhem of a high powered gallery on the west side of Los Angeles. We are both instrumental and occasionally underfoot, but one staff member devotes his day to our safety and schedule. Behind the scenes I watch the monitor for him to retrieve a 12 foot ladder and hold it open and steady in front of the soon-to-be activated sculpture. This is our cue. I take off all my clothes, step into a handmade merkin and pull a pale white plastic mask over my face. It has the mug of a 1950s Barbie, complete with smokey eyes, slim and sloping black eyebrows and pale pink lips. The mouth and nostrils contain small punctures, facilitating my ability to breathe, and subtle slits below the eyelid allow me to quickly consider my new appearance in the bathroom mirror as I wrangle a curly black wig atop my shaved head. I walk back into the gallery with my fellow performer by 10 A.M.

The man is waiting for us at the ladder which my co-performer scales, perching in her seat in the swing, positioned as the second figure from the top. I complete the sculpture as I sit on a stool beneath the tower of five forward-facing nude bodies, stretching from floor to ceiling. Like a freaky or fraught circus, our assembly is sexual, subversive, and strange, we form a totem of nude bodies in a grotesque feminized spectacle. Architecturally, this sculpture is a swing suspended from the ceiling fashioned from Real Dolls drilled and harnessed together with two spots left vacant for me and my fellow performer's real, yet masked, bodies. Our quintet assemblage, from floor to ceiling, deliberately blends real and fake forms (real, fake, fake, real, fake). Perfectly aligned heads and asses give the illusion that we are one solid structure, fused to or birthed by the pussy above us, like a human centipede tower. The dolls hold their legs towards their chests, assuming an explicitly fuckable posture. We sit with our hands resting on our bent knees, our head balanced beneath the ass above us and our ass balanced on the head below.

Just like us, the dolls wear wigs and their empty-eyed gaze mimics our masked stoicism. The dolls are penetrative by design, their slightly open mouths and pussies are a constant reminder of their passive purpose. Their silicone bodies naturally degrade over time, they pill like sticky sweaters. For hours during a much-delayed promotional photoshoot, I watched the dolls be fastidiously wiped down with Goo Gone. The one closest to the ceiling appears child-sized and she clutches her perfectly round breast in one hand, head coyly tilted down, wig slightly falling in her face. The next doll down is made of a lower-grade material, her skin looks jaundiced and she is the only doll with a patch of fake pubic hair. The one directly above me has a voluminous ass which I hold onto to steady the swing while my partner ascends the ladder to take her place in the sculpture. Our pristine stillness and control completes the illusion that this sculpture is made up purely of inanimate forms.

Despite my nudity, I feel unexposed. My genderqueer-ness, my dyke-ness, my thirty years of life and my politics, ethics, and interests are all concealed from those who visit the installation. My nude body transmits the tone of my skin and the certain presence of body hair, but it also reduces me to an object. I offer no animation to my form; I resign myself to the image of a lifeless sculpture, just a shape in space. In daily life I am accustomed to strangers' curiosity or concern about my self-presentation through forms of double-takes, bathroom-policing, and awkward stutters of address between Sir and Miss. I dress with deliberate and playful flamboyance and my self-styling is a vital part of my public persona and presentation. So I welcome the side eyes and double takes from strangers and deliciously blunt, "Are you a boy or a girl?" queries from children. But sitting here, in my naked costume, a wig and face mask are ample disguises for my usually-troublesome gender. I appreciate this simple transition to anonymity, it provides a protective film between me and the gaze of passersby. The mask and wig are enough to render me incognito, making my private experience completely my own.

For twenty-five minute blocks, spanning four or five hours, I watch a stream of people cumulatively shocked to discover that there are two live bodies disguised in this feminine illusion. We sit very still and breathe very shallowly, not because it is implicit in our instruction to be such obedient statues, but because it is rewarding to fool a gullible crowd. The sole directive given by Narcissister, the sculpture's creator, clarifying our assignment, was to "activate it." Our exceptional stillness

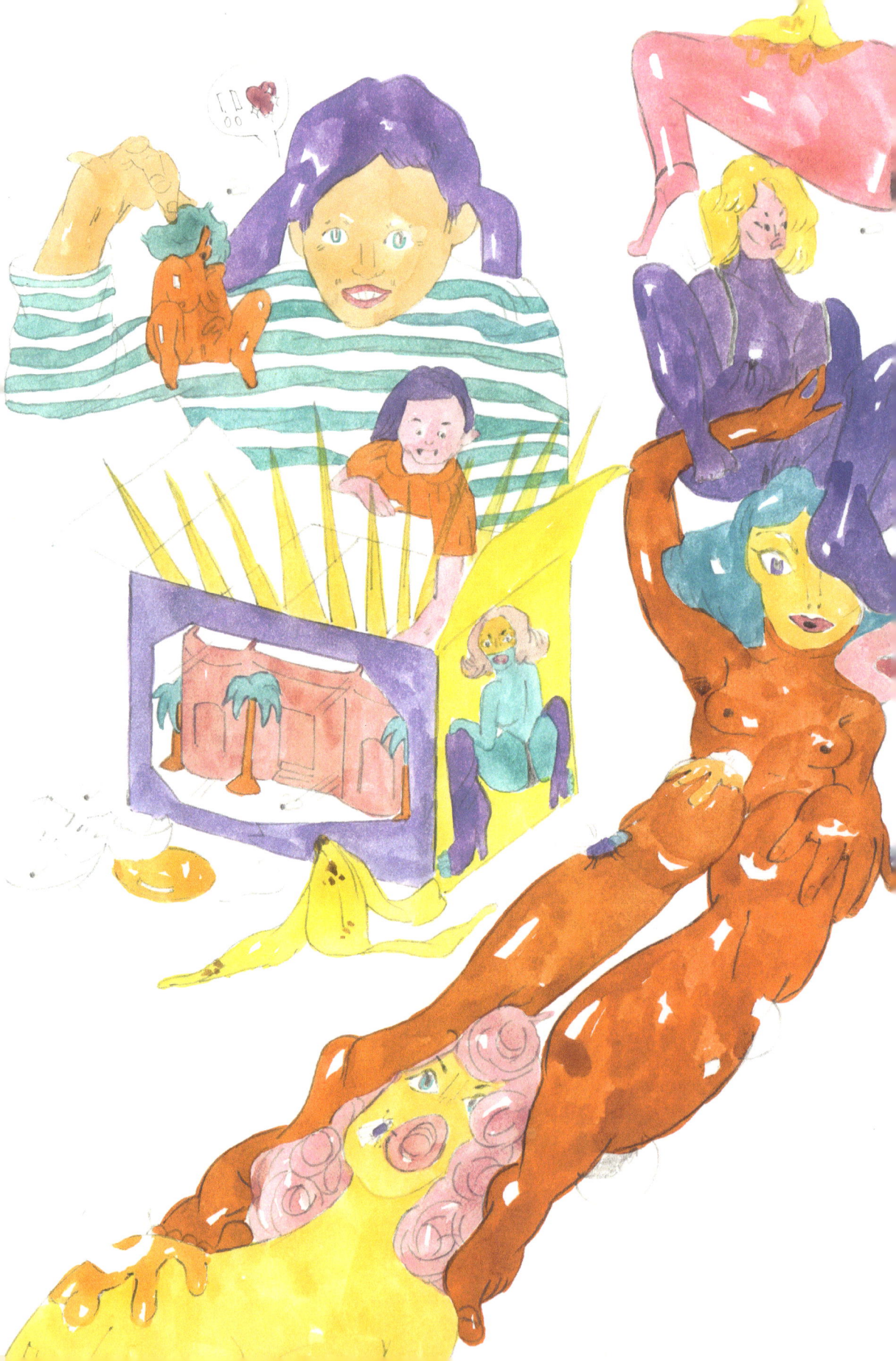

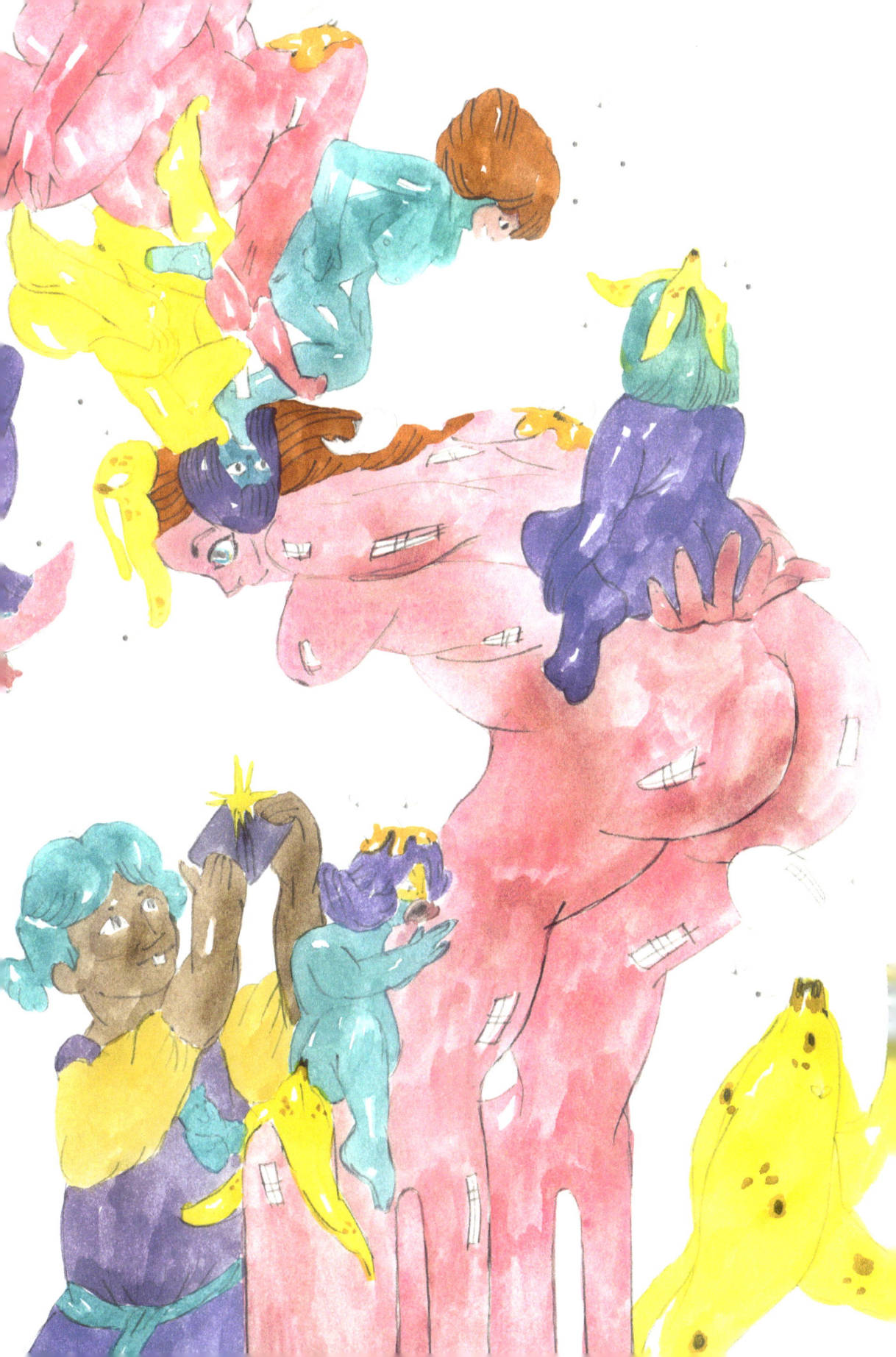

is our choice, making our performance feel more like a participatory game and less like we are an exhibit at the zoo. The expert control I have over my body makes me feel I hold all the cards and have all the power.

Our living bodies, still as stone, offer a vital contribution to this funhouse-esque room of life-sized inanimate objects. We breathe life into it; our very presence animates it. Our bodies bridge the gap between viewer and viewed. We are both inside the exhibition as objects to be gazed upon, and outside of it. We are the only work that goes home at night, the only work with sentience, the only work which walks among "the people." We evoke the rare and magical quality that anything can happen, that in some uncanny world, sculptures can and do come to life. We may resemble the numerous realistic sculptures scattered about the massive and pristinely skylit room, but we breathe, take breaks, drink water, drink coffee, use the bidet, tear clothes off and put them back on before, in between, and after our shifts. We go home with sore backs and return the next day with freshly showered hair. We bring our liveness into our stillness, it's what makes this sculpture such a successful illusion. Behind our performative disguise, we are omniscient and every viewer who eventually discovers the fact of our living form is simultaneously confronted with our totally passive but undeniably comprehensive witness.

This sculpture offers no physical boundary between me and the people who freely enter the gallery, so when I am performing on the ground level, I am concurrently on patrol. I am alert and watching bodies through periods of vacancy and crowding, absorption and boredom. I know my realness will inevitably give me away, that people are sleuthing for the secret, and the only leverage I can mount is for me to sleuth them back. I listen intently to their conversations, I watch how and what and where they look at me. I witness how long it takes for them to realize that part of this tower of bodies is alive. It's a predictable timeline and our necessary breathing is always the clincher.

As proven by the now-vintage feminist works like Yoko Ono's *Cut Piece* and Marina Abramović's *Rhythm 0*, not to mention the voracious sexual assaults on unconscious bodies, there has been and continues to be a disturbing propensity for the public to betray the sovereignty women have over their form. Some kind of cultural compulsion; we still haven't graduated to women having agency over their bodies because we're too busy rubbernecking antiquated assault strategies. The intentionally-passive performative female forms agitate our collective history, allowing unresolved traumas and mindlessly harmful reflexes to rise to the surface, to froth at the mouth, to rise like cream. In these live art experiences, women putting themselves in danger are merely putting themselves in public and perpetrators remain ignorant of their malignant role.

Performing this piece drew unsolicited and unwanted gestures, gazes, and commentary towards my body. I never felt threateningly violated, or felt so unsafe as to interrupt the performance, but each breach, each moment of discomfort accumulated quickly into a deeper dis-ease. There was the mom who urged her adult son to tweak my nipple to confirm if I was real. There was the man with a stuffed cat who stayed for many minutes filming and re-filming his toy cat peering up and down our bodies, animated by his hand. There were all the men who stared as if in a hypnotic trance towards my pubic hair spilling out from behind the sliver of merkin. There was the couple who came too close while discussing my arm hair and the possibility of its realness, "was it transplanted?" There were friends who brought their buddy behind the sculpture to "look at that ass," there were copious males who made me feel unsafe by the amount of time they spent staring, or by their proximity to my form, that after a shift, with surging adrenaline, I would throw my clothes on and remind the gallerists out front to pay attention to us and guard us from threatening viewership.

Savvy art-loving parents come to the show accompanied by their children, most of whom are newly-walking toddlers. While I can't remember one adult remaining unsuspiciously entranced at our sculpture, I recall the feeling that so many children were connecting with our vulnerability. One tiny boy, hand in hand with his much larger father, stopped in his tracks upon seeing us. The father stopped too, glanced at the sculpture, and then took out his phone. The boy stood so still watching us, and eventually told his father the secret he had learned from a patient gaze. "Those two are real." The dad looked up from the phone, at the two of us his son correctly pointed to, and quickly denied his observation. "No, they're not, they're sculptures. Let me take a picture of you in front of them." The boy refused to be photographed until he successfully convinced his distracted father that the sculpture contained both real and fake bodies. Eventually, he succeeded. There are many young visitors like this. They emit the most respectfully curious energy, as if magnetized to our living sculpture. They aren't distracted by phones, cameras, or the virtuosity of our trained bodies, nor are they disturbed by the explicit erotics. They are connecting to something deeper, they are being affected, impacted, and captivated by our dexterous act. They stare without distraction and without an urge for answers. They are engaged without ego, and I am grateful for their unladen vantage.

When I get tired of watching what becomes formulaically predictable audience behaviors, I like to close my eyes and find meditative stillness. I pare down my agenda and pretend that I'm sitting here in a nude disguise unrelated to the paycheck, or audience, or acclaim. It is a necessary act, to shift away from being an invisible witness and instead sense into my performing, working body. I sip up air and sense my form, where I'm holding tension, how I need to adjust. My hips are always the first body part to reach exhaustion, and I send relaxing thoughts to them: with each breath, try to yield a little more to their softness. I make micro-movements in my spine forward or back to ease the pressure on my legs. I move so slightly and slowly I doubt anyone notices. I comfort myself with the reminder that this pain is temporary, that my strict posture always has an endpoint, a promise of rest. In the vast gallery, after a couple rounds on a rainy or surprisingly wintery day, the chill becomes cumulative and inescapable. I open my eyes and envy people parading about the gallery in sweaters and jeans. I feel goosebumps flood my skin, I attempt to suppress the inevitable shiver. I wish for a blast of heat, and I try to conjure the comfort of warmth in my mind. Eventually the shivering subsides, another homage to dissipating discomfort.

I reopen my eyes to a person positioned strategically in front of me snapping a picture of our sculpture. They reposition, reshoot, take solo images of me, step back and take another picture of the whole piece. People come armed with cameras and phones and so fervently document the work. I wonder how long the images will sit dormant in some digital cloud before ever being remembered or referenced. My body has infiltrated their archive, my 30-year-old nudity forever preserved in so many strangers' phones, computers, hard drives. I once didn't recognize my own body in a picture I saw taken of this work, as if the wig, mask and general setting successfully obscured me from my own self-intimacy. I peer out from behind the mask to watch them get the right shot. All these strangers taking pictures of me, taking videos of me, taking selfies with me, taking pictures of their children with me, taking pictures of their spouses with me, taking pictures of their friends with me. I don't do anything. My situation is already posed, but I'm uneasy. What does this documentation cement? What is the point of such a thorough capture? This constant documentation renders every experience mundane, *thanks for including me in your apathetic and endless scroll*.

The shifts intensify as the day progresses. The first few feel breezy and the later ones crawl by. I lose track of how many I do in a day. *Was that the fifth or sixth one?* But I can predict the end of our shift based on the burning sensation in my back from holding so still for so long. I hear the footsteps of our reliable gallery assistant who diligently helps us get in and out of the sculpture after our twenty-five minute sessions. He carries an open ladder to place in front of the sculpture, now signaling the end of the shift. His choreography elicits ecstasy from me on particularly tiring days. I restrain my giddiness as he holds the ladder for the top performer to climb down and then he slides it away, giving me space to finally stand. I extend one foot out and use my arms to press myself to an upright position, moving deliberately to guard myself against imbalance, or in case my limbs are tingly. It is stunning to finally stand. Suddenly I am a giant, huge and tall at this new vantage and some unsuspecting gallery visitors gasp with surprise at our dismount. Sporadically, we receive applause as we end a shift; a kind and extraneous expression of acknowledgment. Most people pause to watch our transition performance: our nude forms retreat to our office-dressing room, having extracted ourselves from the swing of our nude sisters.

It is in this liminality that I feel most virtuosic—the walk from the gallery floor to the back room. Our previously stoic asses, arms and hips are now naturally animated in motion. Arms swinging, legs stepping in front of the other, this is simple pedestrian action and somehow still so captivating. I treasure this uncanniness; that my capacity for oddity as well as grace seamlessly merge in this aspect of the routine. I am controlled; a mystery, yet undeniably real. I love how my form feels in motion, my erect and mobile spine, the weight of my arms against the air, my suddenly-louder bodily desires. I am walking towards rest, towards water, towards a reprieve I need and deserve. I am walking away from the eyes of strangers and towards the I of myself.

Paul Hamilton

I'm a good dancer. I do the movement. A good dancer doesn't need to show much of themselves. I don't get caught up in emotions or feelings or interpretation. I do the movement. The movement tells the story. The movement has everything I need. But in the end, even if some of these positions might be kind of striking or slightly acrobatic, there's really nothing spectacular about them. The work is so bare, and all of the performers spent so much time with it, without direction; it just couldn't help but become ours.

o

The first time I performed the work, it was an opening night reception for the press; a huge party. I remember being very nervous. I remember thinking the pressure was on: to become, to deliver. Afterward, someone told me that Bruce Nauman was there. He may not have watched the entire performance, but I know that he walked through. I never saw him, though, because of the positions (his positions) I was in at the time. I was accompanied by a member of the museum staff who chaperoned me from the dressing room into an elevator, down a floor, through crowds of people and to the space I performed in. I had a guest ticket for the opening night and had invited my boyfriend, who told me that he was going to surprise me when he got there. As I was weaving through the crowd, I saw my boyfriend standing next to where I was about to perform, holding a bouquet of flowers and with freshly-dyed flame red hair. I remember thinking, *Oh my god, what did he do?* He was standing there, just smiling. I didn't have any time to react. I walked directly into the space and got into my first position: a ball on the floor.

It was the largest Bruce Nauman retrospective that has ever been amassed, housed at MoMA in Manhattan and PS1 in Queens. In trying to include some of his movement explorations, the curators had decided to restage his *Wall-Floor Positions* at both locations. All eight of the performers who had been invited were given a video of Nauman. We were told that in 1965, he started out by doing 28 positions, but then by 1968 he had added a whole lot more, amounting to 134 positions by the time he was done. They asked us to harken back to his first version of the work in choosing 28 of his consecutive positions out of the total 134. So if you started at 40, you would go from 40 to 68. We had six weeks to compose and rehearse our selections, and MoMA gave us some abandoned office spaces in the building to rehearse in if we wanted to. There was a lot of back and forth between the performers, because we were allowed to rehearse together, and we would have conversations and show each other what we've been doing. Sometimes I would also work at home, moving my dining table to practice against the wall.

At first, watching the video, it seemed to me that he didn't really have time to enter the space, or to prepare. I struggled to find my beginning, until I saw this ball position (28), which grows into something bigger by the time position 56 comes. I could see a beginning to an end in that. The way I chose to begin, my first two positions were what readied me for the performance. Those positions were not confrontational to the people watching me; they felt internally-focused. I could actually do them while closing my eyes, without having to be seen, and I could use that as the practice in which to arrive. Later, I asked the museum staff if I could add a few more positions, because even at 56, I didn't think that it told the entire story. I felt I needed to get somewhere three positions later to have an arc.

I am used to working with choreographers who have very long processes before arriving on the stage. It can be years, because there is research and reading and dramaturgy, all feeding into the physical manifestation that is performed on stage. With the Nauman project, we had six weeks to rehearse. I felt as though I was learning the work as I performed it. I wanted there to be rigor. Maybe I am always looking for rigor. I want rigor so that I can work.

Getting into position 28 on my first night, I kneeled down and rolled into the wall to a crouched inward position. When he gets into that position in the video, there is a slap sound against the wall. The slap became important to me. I felt like if I got there, kneeled down and rolled over, the audience wouldn't know that something is about to happen without the slap. Even though I am a six-foot-two, bald-headed black guy walking through the museum barefoot, in a white t-shirt and black jeans, kneeling down and rolling into a wall, some people wouldn't know something is happening. They might think I'm just another museum-goer. The slap let them know. It commanded attention. It brought energy to that space, right there.

Performers were each scheduled for two or three out of a total of five performances per day, with each thirty-minute performance followed by a thirty-minute minute break. With thirty minutes to perform my, now 31, positions, the duration of each position might shift a little bit every single time I did it. At first I was very dedicated to rhythm, but by the middle of the exhibition's run, I got into exploring the positions I enjoyed most. The opening position, with the slap, I always liked. I would fight gravity to keep it everytime, clenching my abdominal muscles, sometimes for over ninety seconds, before I released into the next position.

Before the show opened, a woman from the Nauman estate came for a dress rehearsal to see us do the work. I asked her about the noises he would make and whether or not there were certain accents in the sequence. In response, she gave us free rein to interpret it as we saw fit. Towards the end of the exhibition, I felt like I could have walked into the gallery and done 31 positions of my own invention, and that would have been fine. The performer in me wouldn't let me do that, though, and I chose to honor the work I was paid to do. In the end, some sounds I did and some sounds I didn't, but the opening slap remained important.

Two of my favorite positions were the hardest ones: number 33 and number 34. After I've moved off from the wall, I have my left foot against the wall, my right foot spread out on the floor, and my torso

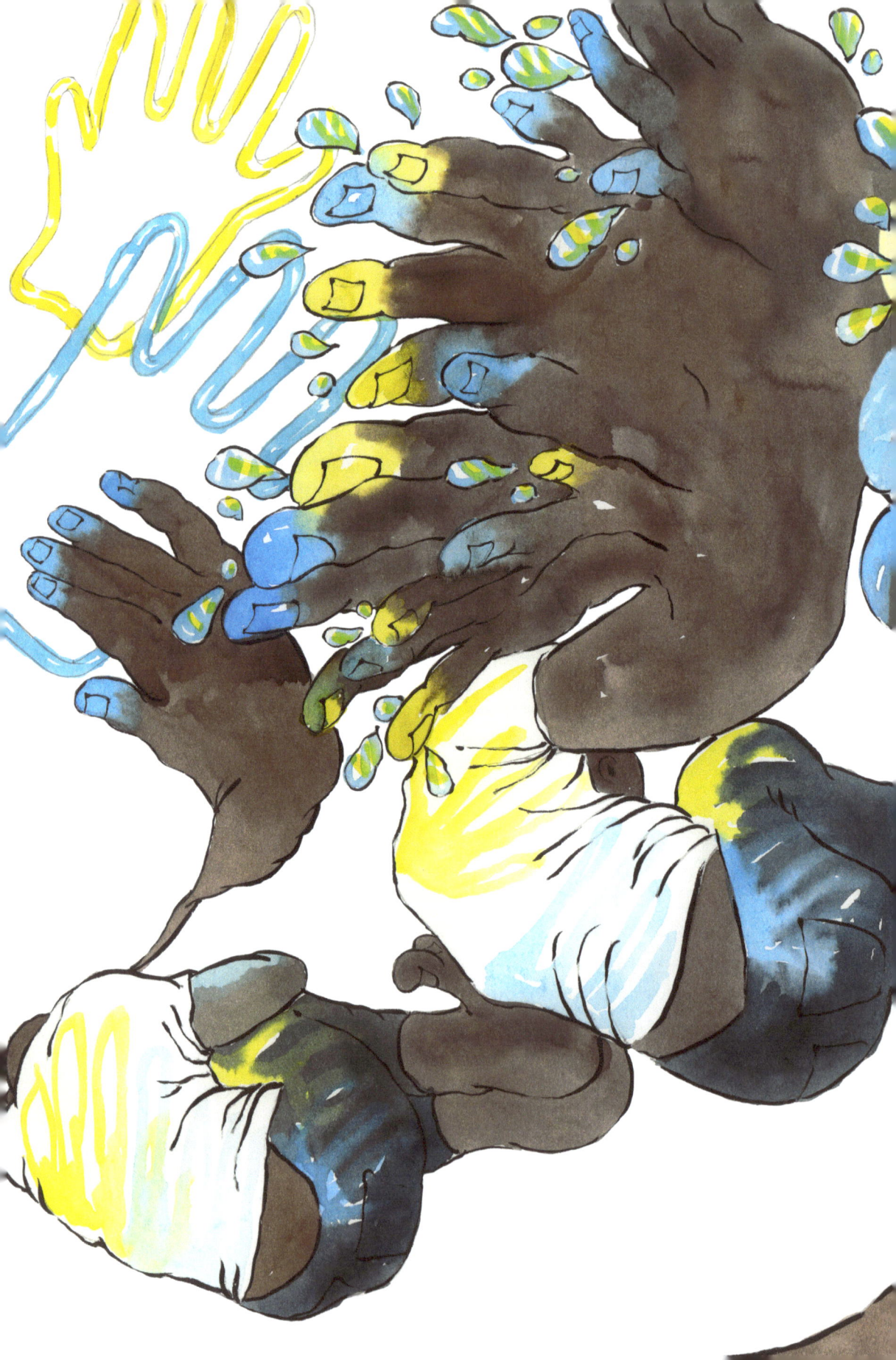

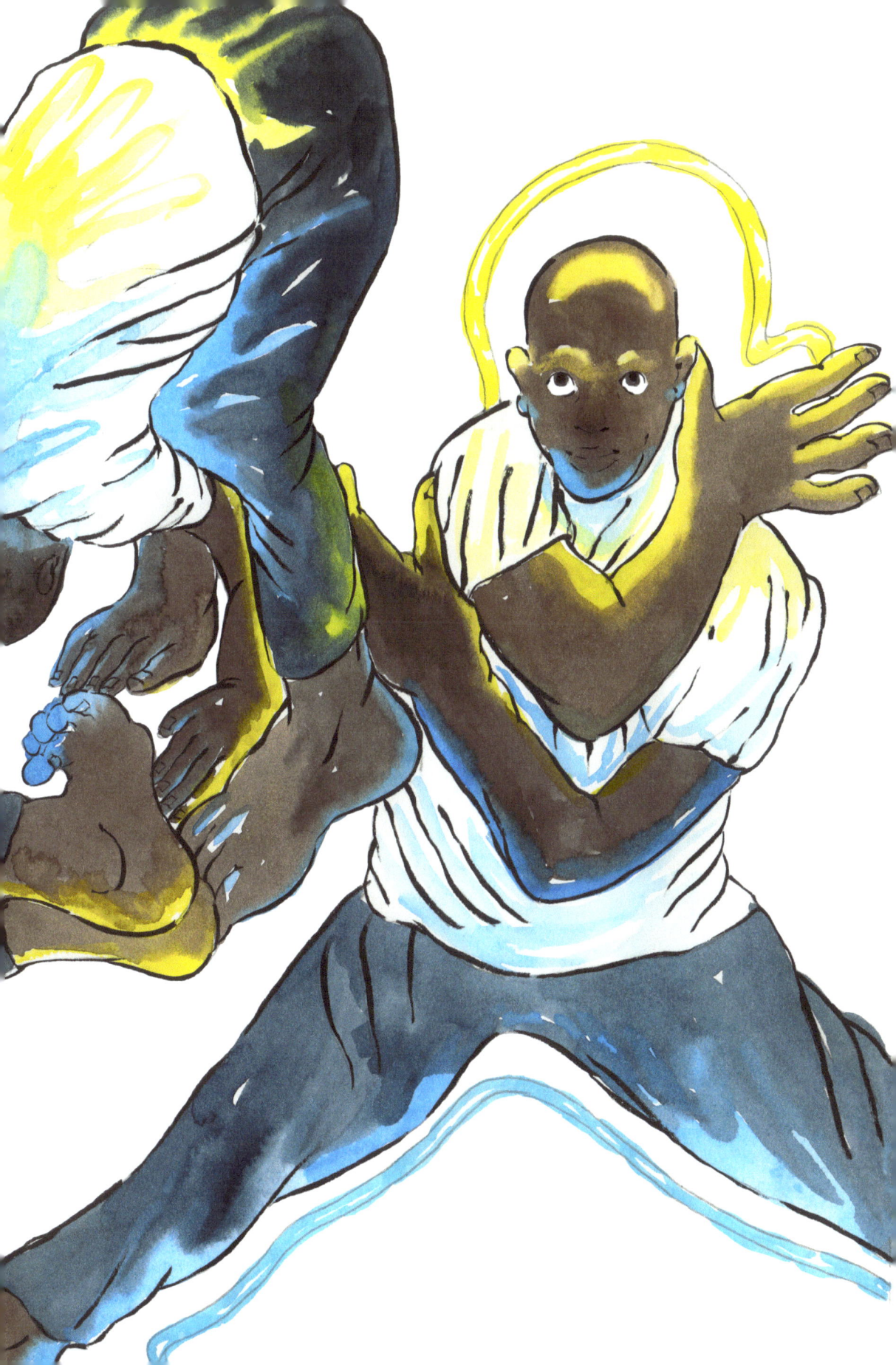

torqued toward my right foot with my hand up against the wall. Doing these positions, I found new respect for Bruce. I remember learning the sequence thinking, "I'm dancing this. I'm a dancer, so I can do difficult things." But when I got to these positions, seeing what he does and trying to translate it through my body, I thought, "Okay, fine, this guy must have hips that are open like nobody else's." I was trying to move my foot one way and contort my torso another, but I didn't have his hips. Even though he was no dancer, the woman from his estate affirmed that he had an incredible body that could do incredible things. From there, he goes into a 180 degree split, and that really tested the stretch of my jeans.

Other positions I liked less, and I would breeze through them. Like 54, which was a sort of inverted fetal position. By the time I got there, I was winded, but my head was tucked so I couldn't really breathe, and my legs ached. I couldn't hold that one for more than thirty seconds. I was glad to get to a standing-straddle forward-bend, toward the end, where my hands were on the ground to support me. In my dance practice, when things get difficult, I plié into them; I go deeper. There were times where my head was against the wall, my arms were out, the back of my neck would start to feel stressed, and the back of my legs would start to give, and then I would breathe deeper. I would breathe deeper, and somehow I would lose track of time. What should have been thirty minutes turned into thirty-five minutes. One day, I went for forty minutes.

During the stretch of the exhibition, I was doing a lot in my life. I was working with Reggie Wilson, who I've worked with for more than twenty years, and I was being asked to do 50 different movements in ten seconds. There were a lot of gestures and head movements and back movements, with everything happening very quickly. Reggie calls it "microwaving." It was also around the time the exhibition started that I met Malcolm. It was strange, I never thought it would continue for as long as it did: more than two years. It was lovely, but it was in the beginning of the relationship when the project started and we were spending a lot, a lot of time together. I was also about to do a project with David Gordon for the Judson Church, and between that, rehearsals with Reggie, time with Malcolm, and now Bruce, I really had no time at all for myself.

Later in my opening night performance, somebody came close and whispered into my ear. I was in position 41, which looks like a downward-facing dog. I couldn't see who it was, but I could feel their breath on my ear and hear them say, "You are very beautiful." The performer in me wouldn't move. I didn't shake. Next, I heard a security guard tell them that they were too close, and I instantly felt grateful.

There were times when I felt lonely, especially when I was at PS1. It was wintertime, and the heating was not so good (as opposed to at MoMA, which felt fancier). I would walk into the gallery barefoot, in my t-shirt and jeans, and the gallery would be freezing. PS1 doesn't have the kind of foot traffic that MoMA has, not being in Manhattan and not being such a tourist destination. Crowds were smaller, and days could be very slow and quiet. Those were the times when I was especially grateful for the security guard at PS1. MoMA had a larger staff with security guards switching in and out, but at PS1 it was always the same person. This person who vigilantly told people when they were getting too close to me; this young fellow who would always, always, always applaud when I finished a performance. I don't know if it was because he wanted to encourage the museum-goers to get interested in the piece, or if he was trying to make them all clap as well, but even when it was just him and one other person in the gallery with me, he would applaud. For the most part we had a pretty non-verbal relationship, but when I did my last performance at PS1, I found my way through the galleries and walked up to him and said, "It was a pleasure, thank you so very much."

A friend told me that when she did a project with Maria Hassabi, museum-goers would walk up and stand next to her head to take a picture. She said that sometimes people would act like they were going to sit on her so that their friends could take a picture as she was lying there. She became close to the security guards, because they were the people protecting her. She told me, "Paul, just make sure you acknowledge the security guards, because they're the ones who are there for you when people overstep the boundaries."

No one would whisper in my ear again after that first night, but I got used to hearing conversations that people would have about me while I was doing the work. "Look at his hands!" "Look at his feet!" "Oh, I like his fingers!" Kids would ask their parents if I lived in the museum. Countless little things were said as I lay on the floor, surrounded by people who seemed to suspend belief that I was a living, hearing human. One time a woman entered the gallery and was so scared when I changed positions that she shrieked, "Oh my god! It's–it's–it's–it's alive!"

o

One of six, I grew up Catholic in what could be considered a safe space for Black folks. Jamaica got its independence back in 1962, and I grew up around people who looked mostly like me. My teachers looked like me. I had the sense that I was a part of the majority. While the colonization of Jamaica had left it rather poor, and they were stripping the island of all of its natural resources, my parents did well enough that I was able to go to an all boys private school and get a good education (which they would later tell me I was wasting away with this dancing thing). There was a certain confidence that I had in myself.

The juxtaposition of my identity as a queer, Black man embodying the work of a very successful, white, American male, in a grand, white building that celebrates whiteness, was not lost on me. With the prevalence of imagery of violence against Black men in the media, I thought about the privilege of my being there, and my simultaneous consternation with being a Black body seen pressed against a wall and motionless on the floor. I also knew that there was nothing I could do to stop anyone from seeing me that way, and that there was a multiplicity of things people could see in my body, going from position to position. I had to trust that two things could arise at the same time:

dehumanization and beauty. I had to believe they would see my execution, my care for the task, my ability, my intelligence and all of the choices that I made in each half an hour; that in those five months, my exploration never ended.

I found myself thinking about *Wall-Floor Positions* a lot during the pandemic. My schedule with the Nauman show was almost always the same. I had a habituated routine with getting my clean, white t-shirt ready, and doing my warm-ups in the dressing room by myself, and then being chaperoned by a staff member to the gallery space where the performance would begin, and when I finished the positions I would be chaperoned back up to the dressing room. There was a rigor in the repetition of all of that consistency. During the pandemic, when I found myself in my apartment, a place where I had spent so relatively little time before, I found a similar rigor. Having to stay in place, shifting between sitting here and sitting there, between the couch and my bed, shifting in the kitchen, never having a break... The monotony became terribly rigorous. I wondered how many positions I went through in a day, before going back to sleep to start again. The Nauman show became the rehearsal process for the confinement of living in quarantine.

o

I've been obsessing over an idea for quite a while now. What if I took Nauman's work outside the museum, and once a day for the next 135 days, I placed myself somewhere in the city, holding one of those positions for at least an hour? I'd be in a subway station, or nestled on a library step, and I wouldn't tell anyone about Nauman. What would they think? Maybe I've become selfish, but I find myself wanting to strike Nauman from it completely. Why does it have to have anything to do with him? The guy does this thing once, and people are writing about him extensively, dissecting his every movement, to the point where they ask eight dance artists to restage the thing he did once, in a museum retrospective that lasts five months. Does that make him a serious practitioner of movement? No, I'd like to think I'm moving on from Nauman now.

Dorothy Dubrule

At work, I pretend to be a museum guard, posting myself behind a wall in the last gallery of a large group exhibition. Whenever a visitor turns the corner and starts to look at the surrounding artworks, my striptease begins. I wear heeled boots that make loud clacking sounds when I pace around the gallery; black slacks, weighty around the waist so that they slip right off once I unzip; a black button-down shirt; a windbreaker with the museum logo embroidered on the chest; and a lanyard with a name tag around my neck. The name tag is attached to a recoiling zip line, so I can slide it out and let it snap back when I am looking for punctuation. I wear a stretchy sports bra, as I like to be able to pull it off over my head without the awkward reach around to unclasp and reclasp. I wear underwear that fully covers my butt crack but doesn't make my stomach or thighs bulge over the elastic.

My breasts and nipples are small. My skin is pale and a little sun-damaged. My butt and thighs have cellulite, stretch marks, and varicose veins. One day I stripped for a woman and her preteen son. Afterward, she approached to thank me for showing him "what a real woman looks like." When everything has come off except for my underwear, I muss my hair and push it up from the back, thrust my other hand up the side seam of my underwear, look a visitor straight in the eyes and say, in the driest voice possible, "Tino Sehgal, *selling out*, 2002." Then I unceremoniously put my clothes back on. When a new visitor enters the gallery, I begin the tease again, transforming from mundane attendant to poised coquette on a dime. If I am almost naked when they enter, I do the striptease backwards: an exercise in tantric dressing. I make $33.33 an hour, before taxes.

At the end of my first shift, my body feels like it has fallen down a rocky hill. My knees are swollen from crawling and sliding on the concrete gallery floor. My hips are sore from gyrating, my lower back aches from standing in heels. It is a Sunday, and I go straight from the museum to the supermarket for my weekly groceries. As I push my cart down the aisles I feel as though I recognize every man's face I see. *That man saw me naked, and that guy. That one, too.* Each pair of eyes bears the reflection of my nipples at the museum. At home, when my partner tries to hug me from behind, I instinctively whip around and grab his arm. To my surprise, even within the safety of a white-walled simulation of sex work, behind the anonymous veil of independent contractor performance labor, the public exposure of my once private sexuality is very real.

I am one of seven performers who does this work. We each work alone. My shifts are three hours long, three to five days a week. While I am on the job, I do not wear a watch or carry my phone. There is no clock in the gallery, and so I have begun a practice of counting every dance, every shift, as a way to measure time. After twenty dances, I know I have about an hour to go. Some days my performance feels full of wonder and whimsy. The striptease is a magic show. With a flick of my eyes, a sleeve falls off my shoulder. A twirl and a wink, and there go my pants. I silently giggle after dropping to the ground like a baby deer and my visitors laugh along. Girls are so clumsy! Other days the minutes drag by, and I find myself wanting to just whip my nipples out so people will hurry up and leave me alone. I shuffle back to the blank wall and wait, eyes glazed, for the next unsuspecting person to enter the gallery.

As I put my clothes back on today, someone asks me if we strippers have all been cast to look alike. After talking more, it becomes clear that they have just seen me, multiple times. Even when one of us visibly drops the veneer of performance and engages in conversations with visitors, the mechanisms of gallery site and museum audience still bends us into the shape of an art object, depersonalized and reproduced with only slight variations. As time passes, I start to question my own uniqueness. *Am I just the product of a design?* Visitors carefully walk around me while I writhe on my back, and as I stare up at them, I find myself in a loop of doubt. I am not sure if I have been choreographed to want to rebel against the sterility of my environment, or if I am genuinely feeling defiant. *What would my rebellion look like? Apathy? Anger? Am I angry that I am earnestly doing the work of inviting my own objectification, or was my doing it always intended to be an exotic tantrum inside gallery walls, crafted to titillate museum patrons?* I could spend the next two hours of my shift internally pawing at this mental knot behind smoldering eyes while I swirl my shirt over my head and slide into a split. Sehgal designed the work to be repeatable, by other performers in other places, ad infinitum. *Am I unconsciously picking up a sixteen-year-old thread of past performers' thoughts, repeating it with only slight variations? Am I losing it?*

A week later, two teenage women sing Shakira songs, dance, and shout affirmations like, "Your hair looks amazing!" while I strip for them. Sometimes I forget that I am dancing naked in public because it feels so good. One afternoon a group of elderly women excitedly speak to me about their relationships to sensuality and aging. Later, I have a long conversation with a stand-up comic about how to keep performing when you know that an audience hates you. Sometimes I actually feel altered by strangers' willingness to be vulnerable with me in spite of the fact that, or maybe because, they nearly see my labia before they hear my voice.

In rehearsals before the exhibition, we were given a crash course in striptease: a glossary of "codes" from which we could develop our individual styles. Masculine stripping, we were told, involves very little movement but takes up a lot of space, whereas the feminine style involves a lot of moving and very little traveling. It was eye-widening to hear this familiar narrative proposed as a physical score. When we began to practice in costume, women were directed to leave their heels on, while men could kick their shoes across the room. Never before had the categories of male and female behavior felt so clearly defined and so strictly in opposition.

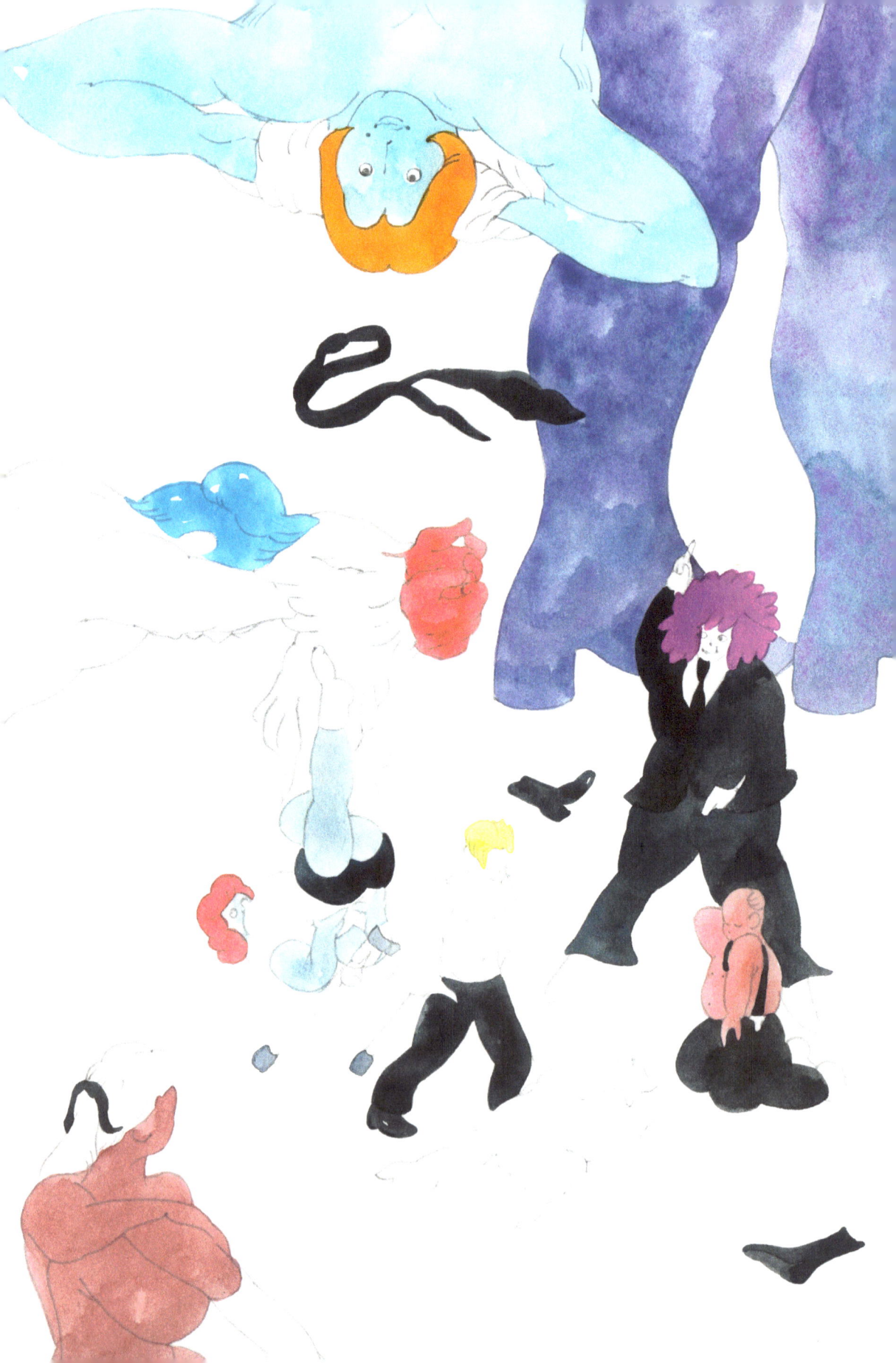

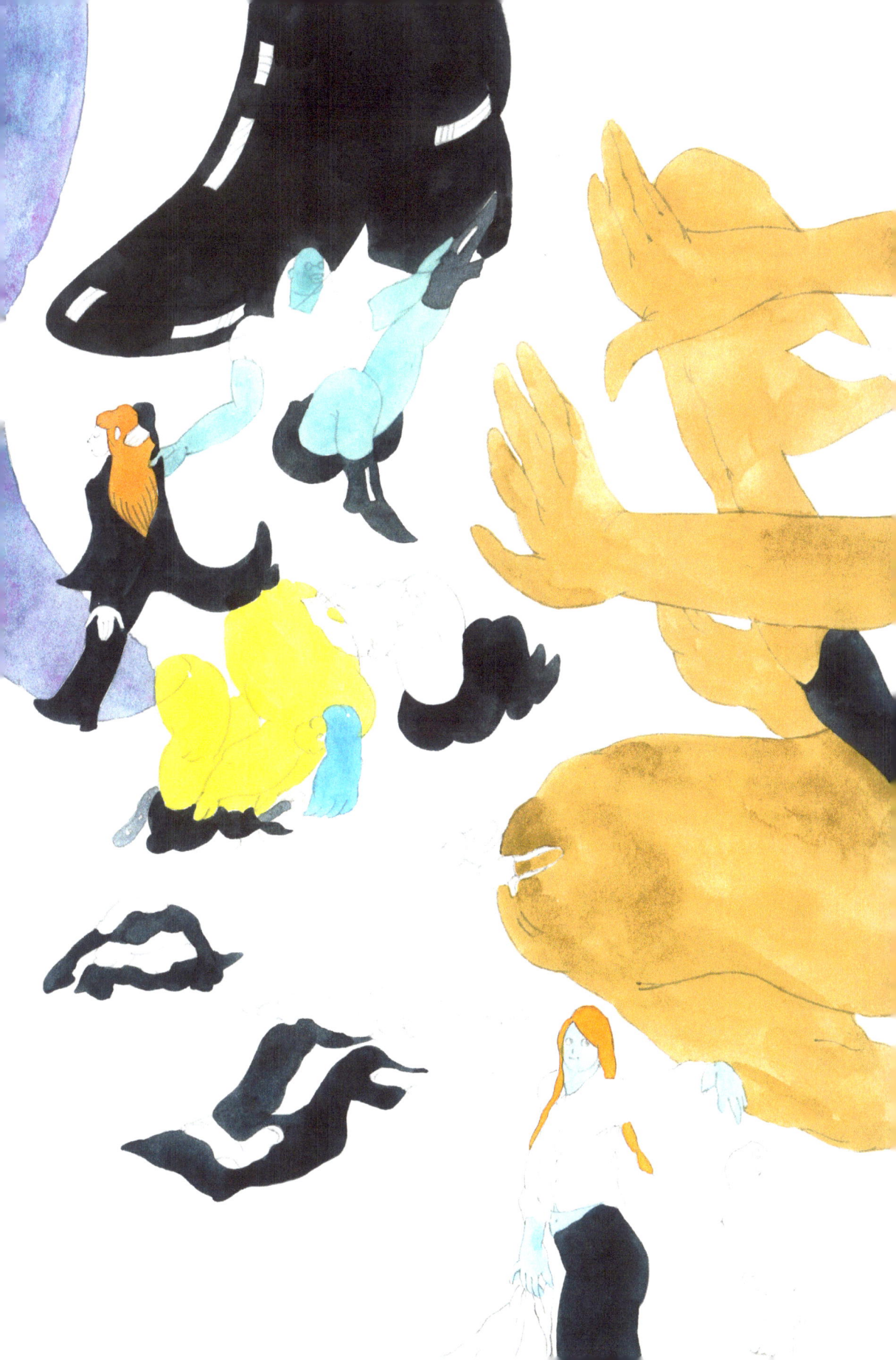

Now a month in, I begin to dance for a man who has his back to me, looking at the installations on the other side of the gallery. As I reach my arms overhead and arch my back he turns around, revealing a smirk that I recognize. I continue to dance while scanning through my memory of recent visitors. By the time I take my pants off, I know I danced for him last week.

Acting on instinct, my movements become heavy and sharp and my eyes narrow, attempting to telegraph to him, "I know your face, motherfucker." I keep my bra on and end the dance—*Tinosehgalsellingout2002*—all in one breath. While it is common to visit an exhibit multiple times when you really like it, surely this is different. I imagine his face as the man in the shadows in the Degas painting *L'Étoile*, where a dancer is onstage, leaning into the foreground, and a partially obscured figure in a tuxedo, her "benefactor," lurks in the wings. But this man is no benefactor. There are no perks to having a regular in a free museum. Later, when another man visits the exhibition several times, using the same tactic of keeping his back to me until I start dancing, I catch on and do nothing until he leaves. Quickly adapting to my refusal, in the following days he begins to wait in the adjacent gallery until I start dancing for another visitor, after which he casually appears. When I ask to have him removed by a museum guard, I learn that his manipulation of the situation is not a punishable act. Even though fellow performers report the same behavior by the very same man, he can't be turned away by the museum staff. He hasn't "done anything."

One afternoon a woman stands alone in the gallery and smiles at me as I raise my arms and slip my foot out to the side, announcing the beginning of my show. I continue to look at her as I unzip my windbreaker and toss it into the air. She laughs. I shift my feet into a lunge, winding up, and then slide myself across the floor, arriving in a pose with my back arched, one leg bent and the other long. After a pause, I lift my fingers to my collar and begin to unbutton, working my way down, looking at her all the while. The corners of her mouth drop as I press my hand into the ground and spin back onto my feet, my shirt slipping off my shoulders. I twist my hips, bending one knee and then the other, letting my bare stomach cinch from side to side. I see a dark cloud of concern drift across her brow. When I reach for the clasp of my pants I know I have lost her. She looks at me, disgusted, as I pirouette on my heel, spotting her face. Before walking out she huffs, "You should be dancing! You should be in a dance class right now instead!" *Where does she think I learned to twirl like this?*

Today a man watches the whole striptease with his wife by his side, each of them seemingly captivated. At the end of my dance, he wants to know what I mean by the closing line. "Selling out? Who is being exploited here?" While collecting my clothes, I say over my shoulder, "I think the idea is that I am exploiting myself." Without pause, he fires back, "I think it's the man." I can't help but respond to that. "Oh? What man?" He blinks with aggravation. "All men! You know, a lot of women use moves just like you did, very persuasively, to profit off of men." "I am not sure how I am profiting off of you right now, sir." At this point his wife steps in with a quick tone, eager to dismiss the mounting tension between us. "Two sides of the coin is all, you know!" She wraps her arm around her husband's waist like a cane whisking a performer offstage. "Yeah, that's right. There are two sides of it!" "Sure." The dance is over.

I have now completed more than fifty hours of museum stripping. I am a pretend sex worker in a high-end simulation. I do not face anything like the social stigma, precarity, or abuse people in the actual sex work industry do. My performance does not reveal to its patrons pervasive and debilitating systemic inequality, the direct connection between the wage gap and the sex work industry, the statistics on violence suffered by sex workers, and the faulty public policy which holds sex workers accountable for their own safety. *Who is being exploited here, sir?*

When I first began doing this work, I believed that, in performing the striptease, I would be participating in an exchange: together we would make the dance, and if the visitor wasn't pulling their energetic weight, I could just lie here like decorative lettuce too. The naive simplicity of this expectation is revealed to me when I dance for an older man alone in the gallery. Upon turning around, wiggling my bra back on, I see that his shorts are around his knees and his bare ass is looking back at me. He lingers that way for a full minute, wanting to sense my reaction. I can't determine what he expects from me now: anger, fear, amusement, or arousal, but all I want to do is disappear. I refuse to give him a response. I am frozen, silent and expressionless. After he finally leaves, a guard advises me that I should be more selective about who I dance for if I am feeling threatened. Yet I feel an involuntary guilt creep in whenever I withhold a dance from a "suspicious" guest.

When did I acquire this compulsion towards obedience in the face of discomfort? If this job were framed as customer service rather than a dance performance, would I be as dedicated to doing it well? Throughout my many waitressing years, I was transactional. I would automate myself in the interest of efficiency, brusquely dismissing any unwanted attention. I could just walk away. As a performer, I am far more eager to please. My training has ingrained in me the belief that there is always more work to be done; I can always do it better. This is how I find myself slowly sinking into a full split even when no one is looking. I am constantly designing and redesigning the choreography, risking injury to enact new feats if an audience member has stayed through multiple iterations of the dance. I want my guests to see the movement as constantly unfolding and unknown. *You don't need to tip me; I want to be good.*

I hate myself the day every visitor leaves me mid-dance, even seconds into my performance. It is a particular feeling to be walked out on while stripping, left alone in a museum with your pants around your ankles. *Have I gained a few pounds? Is it because of this pimple on my chin? I've forgotten how to dance. I'm not as strong as I used to be. I should have smiled more. What is wrong with me that they left? What is wrong with me that I blame myself?* Here I recognize the weighty intersection of being a woman in dance: the recipient of so many gifts of self-denigration. The inexhaustible pull of the never-enough shame spiral. On opening night I hear Sehgal encourage a fellow stripper to think of herself as a sculpture rather than feel ignored. People walk away from sculptures all the time, no big deal. It is freeing to be an art object; there is no shame, no desire. There are no moods, no pain, and no bad days. There are no expectations that a sculpture will respond to or take responsibility for the social conditions it may evoke or produce simply by being there.

Two months into the job, I am visited by a self-identified "Men's Rights Activist." As I lie on my stomach, propped up on my elbows, crossing and uncrossing my legs while languidly looking back at him, he spits, "People like you are the reason why men are losing their jobs! You are ruining men's lives! I suppose if I touched you right now you'd sue me!" He insists that I have entrapped him. I am asking to be touched, dancing and removing my clothes like this. I don't speak this time. Later he returns with a friend whom he tells a nearby guard is his legal advisor. I instinctively duck out of the gallery before he catches sight of me. From outside, I can hear him shouting that he isn't going to leave until I come back. I have to hide in the break room until a supervisor lets me know that the angry man has finally exited the museum. A security guard who keeps me company while I wait him out jokes, "He's like those people that go back to see a movie they know they hate!" "Sure, except I'm a person, not a movie." It feels strange to hear myself asserting my own sentience. Despite efforts to keep it contained, my soft humanness spills out and wants to be acknowledged. I wonder if the guards see me as an allied coworker or just another temporary exhibition.

A friend who comes to see the show asks to hear my "crazy stories" of visitor interactions. He mentions the Marina Abramović piece where she stayed in a gallery for six hours and allowed people to do whatever they wanted to her. "She was almost raped. She was almost killed! You know, people are just animals." I think a lot lately about the lineage of feminist performance artists who authorized their bodies in their artworks as I pace around the gallery, waiting for the next mystery guest to turn the corner. *Back when they made those seminal works, is this what they had in mind for the future? A job market where artists could take their clothes off and get verbally abused in a museum for hours at a time and pay their taxes with the proceeds? I feel complicit in a dangerous fantasy.* In the remaining weeks of the exhibit, I am no longer playing with the composition of the choreography, or my nuanced dynamic with visitors: I am assessing their threat level and hoping they don't notice. This is where the effort of my performance labor lies now.

On my last day stripping in the museum I feel grateful: for the money, the power I sometimes felt, the opportunity to perform the same dance more than 936 times and keep learning from it; for the people who held my eye contact and the ones who raucously clapped their hands for me despite the surrounding silence; for the groups of teenage boys who looked down at their exhibition pamphlets whenever I turned to face them, the parents who calmly talked their wide-eyed children through the experience, the dogs on leashes who tried to dance with me, and the owners who held them back; for my healthy body, which never did sustain any lasting injury, and for the fact that today I am done. I take off my worn-out boots in the gallery for the first time, walk out the door and down the hall, and throw them in a trashcan.

Not a stripper, a museum guard, a sculpture, or a movie, I am walking to my car barefoot and I am going home.

Contributor's Biographies

effie bowen is an artist making performative, printed, and sculptural works which materialize out of gestures of repetition and endurance. effie has performed for Deville Cohen, Ryan McNamara, Jen Rosenblit and Narcissister and has shown work at ICA Richmond (VA), Baby Company (NY), Pieter (LA), Danspace Project (NY), and Ponderosa (DE). effie holds a BFA in Dance from Hollins University and an MFA in Sculpture and Extended Media from Virginia Commonwealth University.

Casey Brown is a movement artist and writer. As a choreographer, dancer, and teacher, her work centers on the body as a site of transcendence as well as connection—to our bodies, environments, and one another. As a writer, Casey creates vivid, truthful recollections of her personal experience through poetry and creative non-fiction. She holds an MFA in Dance from UCLA and graduated magna cum laude from Princeton with a BA in English and concentrations in dance and creative writing. She has presented her choreographies at The Tank, UCLA's Kaufman Theater, the Electric Lodge, the McCarter Theater, and Highways Performance Space, and as a dancer, she has performed professionally with Chantal Cherry, Cuerva Urban Folklórico, Maria Hassabi, and Vic Marks.

Dorothy Dubrule is a choreographer and performer based in Los Angeles. Her choreography is often made in collaboration with people who do not identify as dancers and has been performed in theaters as well as bars, clubs, galleries, sound stages and sports arenas. The content of her choreography draws inspiration from film and community theater. Prior to moving to LA, she danced with DIY performance art collective Club Lyfestile and comedic fly girl crew Body Dreamz in Philadelphia. She has worked with visual artists, musicians, comedians, choreographers and directors such as Emily Mast, Jon Daly, Kate Watson-Wallace, Lea Anderson, Lisel, Melinda Ring, Milka Djordjevich, Narcissister, Tino Sehgal, Trulee Hall and Zoe Aja Moore, among others.

Dorothy received a BA from New College of Florida in 2009, with a concentration in literature and philosophy, and an MFA in choreography and performance from University of California Los Angeles's Department of World Arts and Cultures/Dance in 2016. Her writing has been featured in performance journal *Riting.org* and the San Francisco Museum of Modern Art's digital platform, *Open Space*.

Dorothy was the Executive Director of Pieter Performance Space, a non-profit platform for movement artists, healers and activists based in LA from 2017 to 2022. From arts non-profit leadership she transitioned to organizational operations with a focus on the care and resourcing of humans in the workplace.

Dorothy has served on the board of Grex, the West Coast Affiliate of the AK Rice Institute for the Study of Social Systems since 2018. As chair of the Education and Events Planning Committee, she explores issues of access and application to promote group relations learning.

Eileen Wolf Echikson is a self-taught artist based in Philadelphia. Their work aims to capture the playful nexus where dreams, film and memory collide—where bugs and comics rule the world, and time is of no consequence.

Eileen has completed work for the Philadelphia Museum of Art, World Cafe Live, Vans Shoes, and Philadelphia-based musician Sad13. Their comics have been featured in the 2022 Brooklyn Art Book

Fair, in Partners and Son's annual Philly Comics Expo, and their work has been shown in galleries such as Space 1026, Fairmount House, and Paradigm Gallery.

They are currently pursuing librarianship.

Jessica Emmanuel is a dancer, choreographer, performance artist, educator and curator. She studied Dance & Choreography at the BOCES Cultural Arts Center in New York and is a graduate of The California Institute of the Arts with a BFA in Performance & Choreography. Jessica is the founder of HumamStages and a co-founder of the theater-based artist collective Poor Dog Group. Her work has been presented internationally at the Bootleg Theater, Live Arts Exchange Festival, REDCAT, Montserrat DTLA, Highways Performance Space, Zoukak Studios (Lebanon), The Getty Villa, Interferences Festival (Romania), Baruch Performing Arts Center, The Curtis R. Preim Experimental Media and Performing Arts Center (EMPAC) and The Contemporary Art Museum Santa Barbara. She has choreographed and performed for Poor Dog Group, Heidi Duckler Dance Theater, The MOVEMENT Movement, Ania Catherine, Genevieve Carson, Bryan Reynolds, Paul Outlaw, No)one. Art House and Stacy Dawson Stearns.

Paul Hamilton is a Bessie-nominated dancer who trained at the Jamaica School of Dance and at SUNY Purchase, where he studied with Kevin Wynn and Neil Greenberg. In 2000 he began collaborating with Reggie Wilson/Fist and Heel Performance Group, creating five original works from 2003 to 2014: *Black Burlesque (revisited)*, the Bessie-winning *Big Brick*, *The Good Dance dakar/brooklyn*, *the duet*, and *Moses(es)*. With choreographer Keely Garfield he has created four works from 2005 to 2016: *Scent of Mental Love*, *Telling the Bees*, *Wow*, and *Pow*. Working with choreographer Deborah Hay, he performed at the MoMA for the first time in 2012 in the *Some Sweet Day* dance series. In 2014 he began a collaboration with Ralph Lemon that led to Scaffold Room; he received a Bessie nomination for this and for performances with Garfield and Jane Comfort. In 2018–2019 he performed in two Bessie-winning productions—Comfort's 40th Anniversary Retrospective, and David Thomson's He his own mythical beast—and in two exhibitions at the MoMA: restaging Bruce Nauman's *Wall Floor Positions* for five months in the largest-ever retrospective of Nauman's work; and performing in David Gordon's *The Matter* in the museum's Marron Atrium as part of *Judson Dance Theater: The Work Is Never Done*. An excerpt of his solo *The Sitch* was performed at Danspace Project Gala 2019. Since 2019, he has performed in original works by Melinda Ring (*Strange Engagements*), Ralph Lemon (*Rant*), and Reggie Wison (*Power*). Most recently, he choreographed *The Sound of Morning* for Kevin Beasley as part of the Performa 2021 Biennial. He has also performed with Elizabeth Streb, the Martha Graham Dance Ensemble, Mauri Cramer Dancers, Ballet Arts Theatre, and Headlong Dance Theater.

Allie Hankins is a dancer, performer, and performance-maker working and residing on the unceded lands of the Multnomah, Cowlitz, Confederated Tribes of Grand Ronde, Clackamas, and many other tribes, also known as Portland, Oregon. She is an inaugural resident artist and steward of FLOCK Dance Center, a studio and creative home to Portland's experimental dance artists which was founded in 2013 by Tahni Holt. In 2014, Allie co-initiated Physical Education, a queer performance research cooperative/support group, with Lu Yim, keyon gaskin, and Takahiro Yamamoto. Physical Education hosts reading groups and lectures, curates festivals, and teaches workshops nationally. Allie has danced for choreographers nationally and internationally, including Milka Djordjevich (LA), Morgan Thorson (Minneapolis), Ruairi Donovan (Cork, Ireland), Julien Prévieux (Paris), Tahini Holt (PDX), and Linda Austin (PDX). She has been an Artist in Residence at Headlands Center for the Arts, the Djerassi Resident Artist Program, the Robert Rauschenberg Residency,

Caldera, the Wassaic Project, Ucross, and Centrum. Her website is alliehankins.com.

Kestrel Farin Leah is an interdisciplinary performer and director and co-founder of Physical Plastic theatre project with composer and sound artist Yiannis Christofides. She has shown original work at venues such as REDCAT (US); Human Resources (US); Theatro Polis/NiMAC (CY); and The Vail International Film Festival (US). She is a recipient of the New Music USA award for Physical Plastic's devised work *ALARM* and a Foundation for Contemporary Arts Grant for the solo work *Touch(ed)*. She has participated in residencies including: The Watermill Center (US); Passerelle Centre d'art contemporain (FR); Knockdown Center (US); Theatro Polis/NiMAC (CY); and Cyprus Chamber of Fine Arts (CY).

Kestrel has performed in such venues and festivals as Lincoln Center (US); REDCAT (US); 3LD (US); Los Angeles Contemporary Museum of Art (US); DO DISTURB at Palais de Tokyo (FR); Le Grand Palais (FR); Centre Pompidou, Malaga (ES); Nicosia International Festival (CY); Theatro Polis/NiMAC (CY); Denver Art Museum (US); BlackTina Festival (US); LAX Festival (US); and Fahrenheit/FLAX Foundation (US).

Among the artists she has worked with are WaxFactory theater company, B. Dunn Movement, and LIDA Project; directors such as Paris Erotokritou, Maureen Huskey, Zoe Aja Moore, and Kameron Steele; and visual artists Julie Bena, Patty Chang, Dara Friedman, Emily Mast, Liz Toonkel, and Julien Prévieux.

Kestrel has also appeared on television and in a number of independent/art films.

She holds an MFA in Acting from California Institute of the Arts (US) and a BS in Film and Television Production from Boston University

(US). She dedicated a decade to the Suzuki Method of Actor Training in the US and Japan, and a decade of annual study in Athens under Theodoros Terzopoulos, whose methods she teaches. She has taught for institutions such as Open Up EU; CalArts; and The Watermill Center.

Kestrel's writing on performance has been published in *Riting.org*, *The Theatre Times*, and commissioned for the 17th International Architecture Exhibition of La Biennale di Venezia as part of the Cyprus Pavilion.

Mireya Lucio, born in Puerto Rico and living in Los Angeles by way of New York, is an interdisciplinary artist, writer, director, and performer. After training as an actor (BFA Tisch/NYU; Moscow Art Theatre; MFA CalArts), Mireya developed a performance-making practice stemming from a love of dramaturgy and intuitive assembling. Mireya's work has taken the form of dinners, lectures, walking tours, videos, stage shows, and game nights. Her full-length solo performances unravel timelines embedded with precise historical reenactment into musical extravaganzas: *Brandenburg Gate: The American Hits* (an episodic timeline of US presidential visits and foreign celebrity presence in Berlin, along with renditions of number-one Billboard Chart hits of the day), and *¡Con la boca es un mamey!* (a non-authoritative lecture-cum-personal revisionist history of Puerto Rico as a U.S. colony). Her collaborative practice with Sallie Merkel, *Emotional Labor Co.*, weaves popular culture and academic inquiry into non-linear, transgressive studies of girlhood (as in *Our-So-Called Sleepover, or, Freud and Jung Crash 1995 Through a Ouija Board*), and creates transformative ritual via playful entertainment (as in *The Commons* digital series and the iterative *Witches' Cabaret*). *Conversations with my Descendants via Sci-Fi Space Odyssey*: a screenplay for the stage, a live multimedia performance that fuses speculative fiction, memoir, and post-colonial essay as an embodied future archive of inheritance, was performed at LAX festival in Los Angeles in 2022.

List of Illustrations
All illustrations by Eileen Wolf Echikson

22-23	Chorus of Rotating Heads
32-33	Cocoon Outside Time
40-41	What Do I Need
52-53	Who Owns This Gesture
62-63	As You Were Leaving
72-73	Endless Scroll
84-85	The Slap
94-95	Art Object Shame Spiral

Insert Press has released limited edition prints of each illustration by Eileen Wolf Echikson for *Being Work* as archival inkjet prints on 11" x 17", 21 mil Epson Cold Press Natural paper in an edition of 5 each.

Echikson's eight illustrations for this book were exhibited alongside additional works by the artist in the exhibition *Here Sometimes* at Insert Press General Projects from December 2, 2023 to January 14, 2024.

All works from the exhibiton including the limited edition are available from Insert Press online at www.insert.press